ICT for Curriculum Enhancement

Edited by Moira Monteith

intellect™
Bristol, UK
Portland, OR, USA

First Published in the UK in 2004 by
Intellect Books, PO Box 862, Bristol BS99 1DE, UK

First Published in the USA in 2004 by
Intellect Books, ISBS, 920 NE 58th Ave. Suite 300, Portland, Oregon 97213-3786, USA

A catalogue record for this book is available from the British Library

ISBN 1-84150-061-5

Cover Design: Gabriel Solomons
Copy Editor: Holly Spradling

Printed and bound in Great Britain by 4edge, UK.

Contents

– Contents –

Introduction

Moira Monteith

This selection of forward-looking curriculum developments is organised specifically around the theme of Information Communication Technology (ICT) in education. The context alters in each chapter but the approaches coalesce in several ways. For example, we are all planning curricula which exploit the use of ICT and we believe that feature alone signifies changes in our learning patterns as teachers or students. We do not attempt to predict what technological surprises are in store for us, as previous publications have revealed how problematic this is to do accurately. However, we can with certainty comment on current practice and the implications of research for the near future. The connection between ICT and successful learning will remain as an integral link for a longer period of time than the technology which has brought it into discussion. Additionally, we are all seeking to find principles of practice within an educational environment which is changing rapidly as a result of the use of ICT alongside numerous government initiatives and strategies.

What is happening currently?

Teachers and, indeed, all educators are under pressure indirectly from league tables based on the position of their school, college or university in a range of tests and examinations. Pressure comes also from the challenges of planning to teach effectively and helping pupils and students learn. In this situation, ICT can be seen as both a support and a burden, depending on how it helps alleviate (or increase) the pressure. Some initiatives crowd out others; for instance, the introduction of the Literacy Hour (prescribed time for literacy development in the classroom) did suspend for a while some teachers' willingness to spend time on ICT (Tyldesley, 2002).

At the moment there is an unprecedented amount of training at all educational levels, from primary schools to universities. The outcomes differ according to where a person is on the training ladder. Trainee teachers have to undertake courses in the use of ICT as a way of teaching their own subject if they wish to teach in secondary schools, and in primary they train to teach with ICT across all subjects. Teachers already in post also take part in training but do not have to be assessed on this, as trainee teachers do. Often, part of the training is considered less than satisfactory, by both trainers and trainees. Nevertheless, the training programme is a substantial starter. We hope that the second course will provide a more balanced menu. One thing we can say for certain, ICT will continue to be used in the next decade, but whether it will be whiteboards or laptops or both is yet to be determined.

The place of learning

Libby Jared in her chapter repeats Seymour Papert's claim: 'that the home and the family would be the dominant site of education and learning in the 21st Century', owing to the effects of widespread access to computers and various telecommunications equipment. That must be true, though the linkage can have very subtle effects.

In most western countries we pay more attention financially to university students, then secondary age pupils, then primary age pupils. Secondary pupils in the UK, for example, have more spent on them per pupil than children in primary schools. Hardware, in the form of computers, like the funding in our educational system, has always percolated downwards. During the 90s, very often the oldest machines went down to reception and nursery classes. However, it seems that if we turn the system around we might get rather more value for our money. Thornbury and Grenier (2002) discuss 'Substantial longitudinal research in New Zealand (Carr, 1998) [which] found that the home ownership of computers reversed achievement trends for poorer children. The families who owned computers when their children were younger conferred an advantage on the children in terms of later achievement in maths and English in the early years of schooling. This was regardless of family income; indeed, the advantages were more marked for children from low income families.'

This is a most staggering and exciting indication which may lead us to reconsider the effects of ICT throughout our education system and its links with learning at home. It is true that educational research can only show us what happens in a specific situation or as a result of wide trawls of statistical information. Evidence gives hints, therefore, rather than definite predictions as to what might occur in similar situations, in this case early years education. It seems that computers, well set up in terms of being usable by young children and with appropriate software can encourage a very warm response. This is far from the notion of solitary children hammering at the keyboard to finish games or just using up their time to flip hedgehogs and other creatures about the screen. If all our children become literate and improve at Maths, this in itself would have a major impact on our schooling and subsequently further and higher education.

Use of ICT in learning emphasises or even uncovers what is actually happening in learning situations. It is like having counters or an abacus to count numbers: you can suddenly see (or feel) what is happening – the abacus factor. Home and school together have always had a pervasive influence on learning. You know whether or not you're able to learn in school, where your position is in society, whether girls can 'do' science or boys 'learn' foreign languages. Grammar schools in the UK had the effect they did partly because people believed they supported social mobility. Even though the selection was often mistaken and occurred at a great cost to some individuals. Now, it is possible that future generations may well have a foundation of learning at home which might (almost) be guaranteed to be positive. If that is the case, then the strengthening of home/school links will be extremely efficacious.

It seems we seldom change without considering our own philosophies and beliefs about the ways we learn and teach. (Cordingley, P. 2000, Moseley D. et al. 1999) That being the case, we need to do rather more than just go down to the computer suite for our required slot each week. We have to consider the principles that underlie our teaching and see how they could be accommodated to or even transformed by the use of ICT.

The organisation of the book

Of course, you may read the chapters in any sequence you find useful. It is an interesting feature that nearly every contributor has felt it necessary to explain the context of the teaching and learning situation as they see it. At first sight these paragraphs may look just slightly repetitive but I have not edited them out. They are not the same though similar; so indicating, I believe, how important the writers consider a particular context is to the way we learn. Many of the chapters mention the 'old curriculum' which in part refers to demarcated 'old' subject boundaries and in part the internalised curriculum which we as teachers develop and tend to rely on in the isolation of our classrooms, lecture halls and labs, away from our colleagues.

The first three chapters look at the changes ICT might bring in general to the curriculum. The first chapter sets out the position for change, the second argues for an educationally directed system of learning rather than one dominated by industrial models and indicates areas where the National Curriculum could be ground-breaking. The third illustrates how we assess our progress once we've really started using ICT. The next four chapters look at different kinds of learning aided by ICT: use of a website, computer mediated communication to develop language skills, four studies looking at control of ICT as a learning medium, and the use of ICT in early years learning. The next four chapters consider the planning of specific teacher training courses where ICT is embedded within the course.

In chapter one, I suggest that the concept of modelling may help us examine how our teaching and learning are changing and help guide future development. In Victorian times models tended to be static and certain features of this remain, for instance in a National Curriculum which has to last a given number of years. The primary use of ICT in education so far has been the extremely effective gathering of statistics, so that data collection is now a major preoccupation involving schools, colleges and universities in their collection. The results of sophisticated analyses affect each institution, most notoriously those models dubbed as league tables, but also those which affect the amount of funding for various categories; for example, research in higher education or special needs in mainstream schools.

Teachers cannot juggle all initiatives at once and so tend to adopt a pragmatic model. For many years we have kept to a good practice model as regards ICT in education but an information flow of good practice examples has not changed people's attitudes. The reflective nature of ICT helps us examine our practice. Student and pupil groups have multi-experience as well as multi-ability and use of ICT reveals how singular the individual student really is. Finally, I consider the viewpoint of J. Pickering, indicated by a quotation: 'not to worry whose voice is heard in the essay'.

A positive way forward might be the creation of a database of many case studies, not as exemplars but so that we can reflect on our own progress and recognise where we are.

Martin Owen believes that computers will change what and how we learn, but the curriculum will not be technologically determined. He gives the example of copperplate writing, itself drawn from a previous script used in metalworking, which was required by industry and business and therefore became a dominant feature of the curriculum until the advent of typewriters. Context and tools influence the way we act on the world. Owen uses activity theory to illustrate this point. Our mental practices develop and merge through the internalisation of external activity. Changing the mediation system changes the activity. The outcomes are uncertain so the process itself, in this case the use of ICT, is not deterministic. He doesn't believe the computer is 'just a tool' unless you realise the immense effect tools have on our learning.

He quotes authors who believe digital literacy is linked to a system of social control and neoFordism in the workplace, as industry and business desire an adaptable, flexible, integrated workforce shaped through education. One clear example of these effects is the large number of schools and universities which use industrial/commercial standard software. He is brave enough to critique Papert's book *Mindstorms* where he discusses the concept of the computer language, LOGO. Owen maintains this includes features of Instrumental Progressivism.

Education needs to develop tools for itself. Owen believes we should adopt Freire's policy and practice, of empowering learners. There is much to use creatively in the National Curriculum but this is not happening very often because people have not yet moved away from the 'old curriculum'.

Peter Twining considers how we can assess our progress when we implement use of ICT within our curriculum. He illustrates how very important it is that we think clearly about our policy with regard to ICT.

He believes there has been considerable funding for computers in education but little enhancement of learning. We do not think lucidly about their use because we still hold to the 'old curriculum' and are very imprecise about terms such as 'computer use'. You may agree or disagree with his particular methodology. Nevertheless he gives an outline of all the points we should take into consideration and scrupulously defines the various outcomes we should look for. By having a curriculum model that helps us think more clearly about our educational practice we can heighten the impact of our spending. His model is named the Computer Practice Framework.

Educational objectives often relate to the management of our learning context. Twining examines, for instance, key objectives in a KS2 science programme and shows how subsidiary ICT objectives could be included within it. He cites evidence that computers are more likely to be used when supporting rather than transforming the curriculum. Assessment criteria need to be changed as ICT continues to change the curriculum. In particular, the assessment of the process of learning and group work would tell us more about pupils' and students' learning than the 'assessed' products. That is an important point since it addresses problems of plagiarism and collaboration concerned with use of ICT and addressed in chapter one.

The following chapters illustrate case studies of or commentaries on particular situations which might help us reflect on our own curriculum context as regards use of ICT, plus consider what is happening in contiguous contexts. This book is not intended to provide a narrow outlook indicating models only for our particular situation since ICT is likely to change the entire curriculum. We maintain that it is important to know what is happening throughout the entire curriculum, particularly so when anticipating change.

Libby Jared describes what might seem simple and straightforward: the creation of a website. But this creation has far from simple effects. She writes that constructing this website was 'building a curriculum without walls' and illustrates how new learning skills can be acquired and old ones consolidated by consulting the various areas on a well designed website. However, she is cautious about the shortcuts available to us nowadays from accessing the Internet; we must try 'balancing creativity with the readily available'. Although this is a website for maths, the insights gained from its design and use can be applied to other subject areas.

The website name, NRICH, is an acronym as well as a pun. It was established in what seems an idealistic manner and is available for us all, so 8-year-olds and 50-year-olds can tackle the same problems if they are at the same level of mathematical learning and experience. The website offers attractive learning features, such as online links to the solutions of problems. Studying these as well as trying our own enables us to understand the maths needed to arrive at an elegant solution. This website is one of the few places at the moment where we can reflect 'on the quality of a solution' easily in both classrooms and homes. An archive of previously presented material has been retained so there is a need to become proficient in searching and retrieval – a 'new' and vital skill. Such web-based learning helps collaboration between pupils at home and at school or even between schools. The website also offers a springboard for the consideration of mathematical proof, particularly useful as the National Curriculum has not, so far, improved students' capacity for this rather essential recognition. Jared quotes examples where teachers and learners appear to have changed place, 'a topsy-turvy world' as she describes it. She concludes by stating why she thinks teachers are essential links in learning patterns.

Rachel Pilkington and Peter Kuminek start in a seemingly common-sense way: 'Putting thoughts into words is difficult.' The thrust of their work is concerned with ways to improve students' capacity to accomplish this. They use a particular course module to trial their ideas, so this commentary is an example of 'work in process', something we could aim to do at certain appropriate points in our own teaching. The aim in this particular teaching case study was to develop structured activities with a view to generating reflections on the properties of computer mediated communication (CMC). The production of a meaningful on-task discussion in which the tutor did not participate may be considered an achievement in itself. Pilkington and Kuminek explain the theories from which they take their views of learning and believe that a healthy discourse community should also teach students strategies that are sensitive to relationships between participants. They found evidence of 'deeper student engagement as a result of having to be active and participate' but students did not understand the necessity of having to attend sessions regularly. They present examples of the activities and how the students engaged in them. The students agreed as a group that challenging others to give explanations or justify their point of view was an important skill. As individuals they got to say what they wanted to say, something they felt wouldn't necessarily occur in face-to-face discussion

Jocelyn Wishart examines four research projects concerning motivation and the use of ICT. In the first project, it took a year to see that ICT was causing an impact on their curriculum. Both teachers and pupils noticed changes in teaching styles, particularly the increase in pupils' independence and use of open, flexible learning skills. In the second project concerning the use of multimedia CD-ROMS, teachers claimed these enhanced their teaching and encouraged more student centred learning. Project three followed a history course which was already established and assessed for external purposes and introduced the voluntary use of ICT by pupils from a range of supporting software. The majority of pupils obtained higher grades for their work, and were very enthusiastic about ICT use but a minority of students did not enjoy this. The fourth project looked at learner control, as that might have a bearing as to why some pupils and students were more likely to enjoy opportunities to use ICT than others. Wishart concludes that differentiated training strategies are needed for pupils and students according to how they feel about control of ICT. Additionally, teachers should try to provide greater opportunities for independent learning tasks through the use of a range of software.

The next chapter appears centrally in this collection as work with young children should be central to all education. Deirdre Cook begins by quoting a metaphor of children as biological computers. She argues that early years education has for long encouraged a very principled approach, which includes views on the role of adults and the centrality of play. Such a well-established approach should not be discarded when considering the role of ICT in early education. She looks at the (creative?) gaps and differences in National Curriculum documentation of all four countries of the UK. Parents and teachers scrutinise playthings all the time, so this should be no different when it comes to ICT. Cook gives examples of areas where young children can use software, including personal and social education, art and music, mathematics and literacy. She sympathises with Papert's fear that computers will be used to present 'old' ways of teaching. Literacy boundaries are changing, music and art opportunities have expanded considerably. She agrees with Papert that there must be a balance between instruction, construction and initiation. She emphasises the role of adults in scaffolding procedures for young children (rather as Jared considers the role of teachers) and the importance of home/school links.

The following four chapters describe innovatory teacher-training courses, one primary, two secondary and one for further education students. The course designers have had to operate alongside government directives and their students will be the next generation of teachers, influencing what happens in schools and colleges. They all have had to consider how to combine their views about learning development with external directives.

Babs Dore and Cathy Wickens believe students must see a purpose for ICT use, and in their course for trainee teachers they wish to enthuse students and develop capability rather than skills. They ask the pertinent question, one we must all take on board, as to whether planning should be led by external criteria or should there be higher ideals and aspirations. They describe the planning stage of the course and the relationship of the non-compulsory skills unit with a multimedia-authoring task. The latter proved a breakthrough, encouraging students to enjoy ICT use and share their knowledge. Students acknowledged in their evaluations that they benefited from working in small groups and recognised the value of 'playing' with various applications. Subsequently, the skills section of the course became a series of 'virtual' exercises as the tutors were confirmed in their belief that skills courses do little to develop ICT capability. However, the effect of online learning has still to be evaluated and the writers raise relevant questions both about students' learning and tutors' awareness of what is being learned. Their conclusion – that students need to reflect on their own and others' learning – is one that most of us will agree with.

John Chatterton is writing about a PGCE course for ICT specialists which he helped to design and which he teaches. He states that ICT has two roles: it is a subject and also a medium for teaching other subjects, rather like English and to some extent, maths. Typically PGCE ICT students are a disparate group in terms of age, experience and educational background. He believes they must first learn to work together and share solutions. They map their abilities against the areas of IT in the National Curriculum and work together to select schools for their school experience block. He gives a fascinating account of how they begin by asking how many miles they'll have to travel and end by thinking about what the school teaches and what equipment it has. He accords a weighty significance to group discussion, at first in class and afterwards on computer mediated conferencing. He feels that the discussion leads to better and more thorough learning. The ICT students also work with students whose subjects are modern languages; the former learn something of what they will be expected to do in school in terms of helping colleagues improve their own ICT skills, and the latter learn more about the use of ICT in modern language teaching. The two-way benefits are evident.

Tony Fisher also looks at a PGCE course for intending teachers but this time from the point of view of their teaching subject, in this case, geography. He views the learning taking place from a 'situated cognition' and 'social constructivist' approach. He examines the background therefore of computers in education and more specifically government directives as to their use in teacher training. He believes that we are in a post-modern situation though schools remain modernist institutions and 'mirror the characteristics of Fordist-type mass production.' Education is often seen as one force that can remedy the problems of ailing, post-industrial societies.

There are no ICT specialists in the Nottingham course so ICT is always an aspect of other subject culture. Fisher gives an interesting example of discrete knowledge in map symbols. However, constructivists believe most often individuals do the work of learning and this is dependent on context and prior knowing. This explains why students don't always find it easy to bring their ICT skills, gained in one situation, into play in a totally different one. There is a need for authentic learning tasks. Students decide on their weakest areas in geography and choose one of them, form a group and create a web page focusing on this weakest area. They can, of course, contact other students who are more expert in this subject area. The second task is to observe a geoskills package used by pupils during a lesson in school. He concludes that student teachers' learning about ICT cannot but reflect the particular social practices they encounter in their PGCE course.

Stevie Vanhegan is writing about students training to teach in further or post-16 education. This has been seen sometimes in past years as quite a separate education area and this is evidenced to some extent by the fact that they have different standards to meet and indeed, use the term IT instead of ICT currently, with different levels of skills and competences. However, over recent years sensibly the division has become rather more blurred. Pupils in secondary schools can now attend FE Colleges earlier than sixteen, and many adults gain access to higher education through particular courses in Colleges.

FE lecturers now have to be qualified to a national standard and must be able to teach all key skills (one of which is IT). Vanhegan looks at student evaluations of the IT component as recorded in their course journals and shows how students responded to and made use of the programme's IT component for their professional development. She outlines the standards required for the PGCE students from the point of view of being future college lecturers. They needed to become confident in the use of IT and capable of modelling good practice in this key skill area. The group had a tremendous range of ability and experience, since it included students with very little indeed and others with degrees using IT who were planning to teach it. All students had to progress beyond their level of skill at point of entry. Peer group support was encouraged. Anxiety appeared to be a factor which affected the less able, thus reiterating the points made by Wishart on control of learning. The more advanced students appeared to enjoy the sessions more. While out on placement or college experience their attitudes towards IT became more instrumental, shifting from learner needs to user needs.

References

Carr, M. (1998) *Assessing Children's Experiences in Early Childhood: Final Report to the Ministry of Education*, New Zealand

Cordingley, P. (2000) 'Teacher Perspectives on the Accessibility and Usability of Research outputs'. BERA Conference. Disseminated by the Teacher Training Agency, London

Moseley D. et al. (1999) *Ways Forward with ICT: Effective Pedagogy using Information and Communications Technology in Literacy and Numeracy in Primary Schools* Newcastle upon Tyne: University of Newcastle upon Tyne, (ISBN 0 7017 0086 6)

Thornbury, M. L. and Grenier, J. (2002) Joint Attention: Adults and Children Playing with Computers in Monteith (ed) *Teaching Primary Literacy with ICT*. Milton Keynes: Open University Press

Remodelling Education

Moira Monteith

The concept of flux has existed ever since Heraclitus put his leg into a river in 513 BC to show people how things keep changing. 'Management of change' in education has been discussed perhaps for three or four decades. Recent research papers and government initiatives, particularly those concerned with the use of ICT, pelt us with facts on the inevitability of change. (Undoubtedly ICT brings changes, some expected, others quite unexpected. This chapter suggests ways of using IT to help us understand what is happening within our classrooms, to gain knowledge of ourselves and our teaching.)

Modelling is a learning strategy included within National Curriculum guidelines and considered conceptually useful in terms of planning, deciding which techniques to use in problem solving, and developing new designs and ways of looking at past events. Oldknow and Taylor (1998) propose two definitions: 'the development of a hypothesis to explain the connection between variables in a system … in a vaguer sense the word "modelling" is used synonymously with "What if..?"' I suggest modelling may provide a useful strategy for looking at our own practices in teaching and learning. In particular, our behaviour with ICT reflects our practices, both in the use of ICT and whatever else we do in education. ℚ — Analysis

Oldknow and Taylor's definition above indicates that we might be dealing with one or several hypotheses to explain the connection between variables. However, many computer-based models are in fact the hypothesis stage and suggest what might happen with a given set of variables, perhaps sequentially changing the variables. Such models achieved public prominence in the UK during the 2001 outbreak of foot-and-mouth infections in livestock. Various outcomes were plotted and results shown on national TV newscasts. One particular model which involved the quick slaughter of herds diagnosed as infected, appeared to have a considerable effect in terms of how the outbreak was dealt with. Since speed was one of the important factors in this model, suspect animals were slaughtered as quickly as possible, some animals before subsequent tests proved the diagnosis to be mistaken. Similarly, within most models, certain features will become foregrounded and their prominence can skew what happens when we attempt to replicate the model in a slightly different context.

The model previously cited, concerning the foot-and-mouth epidemic, implied quick action. Some models seem comparatively static, particularly if they are considered the 'ideal'. In Victorian schools, children had 'model' lessons describing, for example, exotic animals when a model of the animal would be shown to the class. In a Derbyshire village school the inspectors of the day found fault with a school's resources: there were insufficient models to give children opportunities to understand the world outside their county. The governors clubbed together and between them bought a few more models, including one of a whale. In a school with no TV, few photographs and not many books it must have been difficult for children to imagine what whales are like. The model in this case remained the same for succeeding intakes of children over many years, enabling the children to widen their knowledge of the earth and its creatures. However, it was only one model of one kind of whale. A prescriptive model often implies a static viewpoint. The National Curriculum cannot be the same in all the contexts of all the schools there are in England but we have endeavoured to make it so. There are signs, however, that this policy is changing and schools will be able to look at curricula in a more independent manner, developing a number of different curricular models.

Information technology and history

Using different variables we can plot the past in a range of models. We do not need to alter facts as Orwell suggested might happen in his novel *1984*. We merely foreground one or more specific features in which we are interested. Simplistic but fascinating. Early accounts of history were modelled on the life and death of various kings and queens. Economic history, on the other hand, considers factors other than just the sovereign's life and his/her management skills. If we examine history from the point of view of where information came from and who knew what about its flow (Rodriguez and Ferrante, 1996), then we end up with a rather different view of what was and might be happening.

In agrarian societies, information tends to come from the top heirarchically, and is passed down through social layers. Knowledge held by those at the bottom of the social pyramid, though essential for their survival, perhaps about which herbs to eat, how to cultivate certain foodstuffs, was often neglected in the past by those at higher social levels, sometimes to their cost. Usually there are few past records of what people at the bottom of the social pyramid did know.

Social layers change when industrialisation occurs within a country. The people with new knowledge are those who understand how to run and maintain factories, mills, mines and other industries. Managers become important, receiving information from above, passing it down and training people to work in new ways. Still the information flow remains predominantly one way and problems experienced by people at the bottom are never realised or even known by those at the top. Strikes and withdrawal of labour occur, even riots and rebellions, situations which might have been avoided had their employers and governments understood what was happening.

Currently, we are living in what is claimed to be an Information Age, where information is deemed pre-eminently important. Middle management has lost some of its power since top social layers can communicate more easily with those way beneath. Consequently, there are fewer layers to the now flatter social pyramid. Those without appropriate information can fall outside the model altogether and become a new version of underclass. Sovereigns no longer seem very important as such, and even those people apparently running multi-national companies are only as good as their information. Consumer groups can wield power through the knowledge they have gained of certain products or results from certain industrial processes and, by disseminating this information, they can alter the sales (and thus the processes) of the industries concerned. Within such a world view, information is king.

We can discuss at length the differences between information, knowledge and wisdom and clearly they are different. There is no doubt, however, that appropriate information and intelligence of what is happening are extremely important in social, educational and employment terms. The direction of the information flow is also significant. Global information may have made the world seem a smaller place but if governments don't know how their country is perceived by others, or how certain of their actions are applauded or disliked a chink is opened in their defences. The problem in government and management terms seems to be that the governors and managers can dictate only the information they send out. They are still left with a gap in their knowledge if they don't collect all possible information, including the needs and knowledge of those people at the bottom of the heaps. The term we currently use, 'information technology', first appeared in the Harvard Business Review in 1958. In half a century the collection and storage of information has become one of the main preoccupations of all major governments.

Foregrounding ICT in education

If we run a model of educational development foregrounding ICT, the major effects so far have occurred outside the classroom. These have been concerned with the implementation of ICT in school administration and the collection of information about our education system. Government-run databases contain a wide range of details about schools, from pupils' average reading ages, to the provision of curricula on 'personal health and social education', and details about staff and school buildings. Some schools, parents and/or governors have claimed that specific data has been incorrect because the questions asked were insufficiently contextualised. Many of these criticisms have been heeded so that more subtly worded questions were developed and sophisticated analyses directed. A very recent OFSTED report gives an example of this: 'At the end of Year 9 in tests in English, mathematics and science, the results in 2000 were well below average compared with those for all schools, though broadly average when compared with results in schools with similar intakes.' A similar statement is made about Year 11 students as well as a statement about the attainment of students when they come into the school at the age of eleven. Just to make those statements alone requires effective national databases plus the requirement of all schools to make results available and, indeed, to help with the collection of requisite data.

Similarly, in a survey by BECTa on the relationship between ICT and primary school standards, October 2000, p14:

> The correlation between ICT resource grade and the summative grade given for pupil attainment at Key Stage 2 was calculated, based on the sample of all junior schools[ie those inspected].The correlation was found to be 0.07. This is statistically significant (that is, we can be confident that it is not simply the result of chance sampling variation).

This indicator led to a statement:

> Key Finding: The better the ICT rating of a Primary School, the more likely it is to be amongst above-average schools for all core national tests at Key Stage 2. Statistically, there is a significant positive correlation between the schools' Ofsted ICT resource grade and their grade for overall Key Stage 2 attainment. This trend is consistant across all core subject areas.

This publication of data, *A preliminary report for the DfEE on the relationship between ICT and primary school standards – an analysis of Ofsted inspection data for 1998 – 9*, (BECTa 2000) includes a methodology section, so that readers and researchers may interpret the results more effectively and know exactly how the figures were arrived at. These details indicate both the strengths and the weakness of such models. It certainly looks as if we should regard favourably schools with satisfactory (or above) ICT facilities. However, we must remember that we are looking at one factor only (in this case ICT) and the social organism which is the school must certainly have far more subtle workings than the relationship between ICT resources and school test results.

The use of computers and other allied technology has helped considerably in successive governments' centralisation of the curriculum, both in collecting information and delivering printed curricular materials. Examination results have been available to governments for many years; but in the past, for example in the 1950s, the majority of pupils did not appear on these results because they never took any public exams after the age of eleven. (The exam popularly known as the eleven-plus which decided in the main whether or not a child went on to a grammar school). Trawls for information these days can include all schools, with a view that some data at least will be used comparatively.

Data used comparatively can of course lead to outcomes such as 'League Tables' of school results. The schools at the bottom of the list are probably selected for that position through a number of variables, some of which the school may not control. For example, if we take into consideration the statistical finding that boys tend to achieve less well in terms of their literacy development than girls it should come as no surprise that schools which have more boys as pupils than girls are more likely to fail an OFSTED inspection. An analysis of several hundred OFSTED inspection reports revealed that schools where there were 10% more boys than girls were more likely to be put on the failing list. Chief Inspector Mike Tomlinson stated, 3rd October, 2001: 'We know that once the proportion of boys and girls reaches a greater than 10% difference, then you have got a problem on your hands'. The account goes on to state that the allocation of school places may be affected by this information. Now that the infrastructure for collecting educational data is in place and computers exist to run analyses we need to ensure that more complex models are developed than 'league tables'.

Certainly, some statisticians who work in the field of education, such as Eugene Owen, (2000) at the National Center for Education Statistics, Washington, US, believe that comparable studies of schools and education systems can help all of us see what works best. We can attempt to follow that success, if we wish, by using what he calls 'intellectual capital', that is the knowledge gained from other educationalists' experience. He quotes as one example evidence from the Third International Mathematics and Science Study (TIMSS), which included video study of mathematics classrooms:

> Seventy-six percent of Japanese teachers reported that they meet at least once a month to discuss curriculum, compared to 60 percent of U.S. teachers and 44 percent of German teachers. Moreover, it is a regular occurrence in Japan for teachers to go into each other's classrooms to observe or be observed. Sixty-four percent of U.S. teachers have never entered another teacher's classroom for that purpose, and similarly, 61 percent report that they have never been observed by a peer. Even the physical structure of schools in Japan supports teacher collaboration: schools have large teacher workrooms, where each teacher has a desk nearby his or her colleagues who teach the same grade or subjects. The widely understood culture of privacy and individual entrepreneurialship in American classrooms is in stark contrast to Japan in which good ideas are expected to be "handed down" from one teacher to another.
>
> (Owen, 2000)

It also seems likely that more international indices will be made available. The Human Development Index (www.undp.org/hdro/) already includes literacy rates as one of the indicators of development within any country and may well go on to include other educational data in the future. It currently includes the number of years children attend school in each country. None of this would have been possible without the collection, organisation and dissemination of vast amounts of electronic information.

ICT in the Classroom or The Pragmatic Model

When several initiatives come on stream at once, particularly those which are government funded, many teachers find it difficult to keep all of them going simultaneously. For example, when literacy development appeared to be the major goal, that was the goal teachers in Primary Schools aimed for. This meant that ICT, as another initiative, took a back seat. Steve Higgins and David Moseley began a project in Newcastle schools to encourage better achievement in literacy and numeracy using ICT, so they sent out a questionnaire in Autumn 1997, concerning the use schools made then of their ICT facilities. A year later, they asked for an update:

> ...this indicated rapid change in some areas, particularly Internet access. 37% of schools were now connected (usually one computer, probably in the office or possibly the library). More importantly, however, daily use of computers in class had declined – some of the teachers we worked with reported that this was due to the introduction of the literacy hour and what they felt was appropriate in the light of the literacy strategy guidelines.
>
> (Higgins and Moseley, 2002)

Teachers have been extremely pragmatic and delivered results according to their estimate of what the current government department wanted. They rather naturally put their trust in tried-and-tested methods with which they felt confident rather than an area such as ICT with which they generally felt less at ease and which as everyone admits, can sometimes present practical difficulties not only in terms of equipment but also of class management.

> We found that teachers provided less feedback to pupils during these 'Literacy plus ICT' lessons and carried out significantly less marking of pupils' work. It seemed that when the teacher's attention was divided, the lesson became less interactive for the whole class. In most cases the teacher acted as helper for the children using computers, typically spending half of the time available with those children. Because of this, the quality of teacher-pupil talk with the class as a whole seemed negatively affected, in that the teacher was less likely to ask pupils to expand on their answers and to engage in extended talk to develop understanding. Plenary review sessions were sometimes omitted and when they did take place, teachers asked fewer questions.
>
> (Higgins and Moseley, 2002)

This observation indicates that teaching one subject area through a specific medium, in this case ICT, might result in the dilution of the teaching focused on that subject area. If we imagine a reverse situation, ICT taught through literacy skills, a similar result might well be the case. This should give us pause for thought. Graham Jarvis (2001) very sensibly states: 'The first thing to realise is that confident and competent use of computers takes time to achieve.' He goes on to say:

> In the desire to make our teachers, trainees and pupils computer able and literate perhaps we have overlooked computer cognition. We are all familiar with ... "starting where the learner is". Perhaps it is a view of IT (and ICT) which would be beneficial and meet the needs of both teachers and learners. The emphasis on "skills tests" as a measure of trainee competence indicates an over-simplistic view of a complex problem....Basic computer competence may be necessary but there is a need to enthuse and break down negative attitudes as well as addressing issues of pedagogy.

Jarvis is stating a basic educational maxim, that of beginning where the learner is. His aim is 'computer cognition,' by which he means 'a more fundamental knowledge and understanding of the workings of the computer and how it might be used either in its own right or as a support to teaching and learning. To begin to have knowledge and understanding of its potential.' (Jarvis, 2002) No doubt many of us would like to debate his definition and even the term 'computer cognition' itself. Nevertheless, he has put into words what we are surely all aiming for. Current computer literacy or computer competence courses may be a starting point for future enthusiasts, but any learning model we employ must also build in the valuable asset of teachers' pragmatism. 'Enthusiasm' and deep-seated 'negative attitudes' need careful thought, however, before we arrive at a model which will accommodate them both.

The Good practice model

For a number of years ICT in schools existed as a voluntary activity espoused by enthusiasts. Encouragement to others meant, in effect, a discussion of examples of good practice. The National Council for Educational Technology, (NCET), the forerunner of BECTa and itself a combination of previous organisations which had been formed to encourage ICT in education, built up considerable expertise in finding and disseminating examples of good practice. Businesses such as British Telecom have given grants to specific schools for ICT and organised award sessions where successful schools talked about their projects. Enthusiasm therefore was an important factor and keen teachers and lecturers took up computers and/or software that was given or lent them or which they themselves were particularly interested in. Books catered for enthusiasts. For instance, *New Horizons in Educational Computing* (Yazdani, ed. 1987) included chapters on using the computer language Prolog in the classroom, chapters which would appeal to only a minority of those interested in using ICT, themselves very much a minority in the classroom. The significance of the ICT enthusiast resulted in ICT work being linked with a few people in a school. If one or two members of staff left, a flourishing ICT school could disappear overnight.

Even when computers became far more widespread, ICT remained a minority interest. Exemplary practice does not produce quick results or encourage wide dissemination of new practices. The 'good practice' model, though a very creditable enterprise does not appear to bring about a major change. It is not enough to promote an information flow concerning good examples, and hope that that in itself will bring about 'computer cognition'.

Teachers' views of how research might help them

According to a paper made available by the Teacher Training Agency (Cordingley et al. 2000) teachers want short summaries of research so they can decide if they wish to pursue certain evidence further, video clips and 'vivid and detailed case studies'- in fact a 'good practice' model. However, the authors express concern about 'how easy it is for enthusiastic recommendations of particular strategies to sound hectoring to a teacher audience.' (Cordingley et al.:3) Quite possibly, those of us who are enthusiasts do not realise sufficiently the hectoring implications of our 'easy to follow' case studies.

Cordingley et al. note the position most teachers find themselves in: they have to make quick decisions usually by themselves in a room separated from other members of staff. 'Internalised knowledge is hard to discuss and the isolation of the classroom experience is reinforced. Grounding research outputs in this reality is important to its credibility.' Following on from this:

> '...it is only when their knowledge and beliefs about their subject and their pupils have been explored alongside their actions that profound differences that affect learning start to emerge. Detailed analysis of both actions and beliefs in the "Effective Teachers of Numeracy" report seems to help teachers think about how to embed change deeply into their practice.'

It does at least seem reasonable to give time and help to teachers to consider what their own philosophy is and also to discuss it with others, so that we can all learn by this process. This might be the way forward towards 'computer cognition', so that teachers can become enthusiasts themselves instead of only imitating what other enthusiasts have achieved. Overall progress might be slower, but also much more profound.

The possibility of visiting other teachers in their classrooms now seems popular: Malcolm Chesney, Head of Moat Farm Junior School, one of the Beacon Schools Initiative, and incidentally praised for its ICT, stated December 2000: 'the opportunity to see other teachers put initiatives into practice is invaluable and far more useful than the usual methods of in-service training, which generally involve a course, a powerpoint presentation and a lot of theory. "I'd rather see people go out and spend a day in another school than go on a course"'. Nevertheless, it is important not to allow any sharing of experiences to slip into a 'good practice scenario' only. We need to engage with our own philosophies as to learning and classroom management and consider any visits or exchanges in the light of this engagement.

The reflective capacity of ICT

In order to promote learning change, teachers should be able to assess where they are themselves in the use of ICT; this should not be too difficult if we consider the reflective nature of ICT. I am not drawing any inferences here as to what we think about computers and their relationship with us, such as you might find in *The Second Self* (Turkle, 1984). I am suggesting that use of ICT reveals the concrete effects of our policies and behaviour, rather as an abacus does for counting. It concretises what happens in classroom management for instance, or clearly helps us see problems in an 'objectified' manner. Focusing on computers may in this way help clarify our attitudes about learning in general.

ICT has shown us how we revert to previous procedures (or underlying habits) all too easily. For instance, in the past children made 'fine' copies of their handwritten work to put up on the classroom walls or for other presentation purposes. Many have been similarly encouraged to use expensive computers to make 'fine' copies or to perform 'drill skills' exercises rather than use ICT creatively. We find a similar feature in employment practice, where IT can be used to check up exactly how long employees have been working at their computers and even to check on what they are saying in their emails (as opposed to somewhat freer coffee break chat). Martin Owen in his chapter discusses this reversion to earlier forms of staff management in his comments on neoFordism. Presumably a tendency to hark back, to rest on the strong support of custom and practice, is always present; it is just that ICT makes it more obvious.

Research into the use of ICT in education reveals further aspects of our behaviour than just our use of ICT. It helps us see how we cope with change and even, perhaps, the inevitability of change. Even if we subscribe to the notion: 'If the thing works why fix it?' we come to realise that events and technology do not wait for us. In an evolving situation, such as we find in education, complete reversal of practice is well-nigh impossible. There is only so much change that people can be encouraged to take up productively at one time, as shown by Higgins and Moseley (2002). To explain the current situation where various stages of ICT implementation co-exist, Thomas Carroll (2000) takes the metaphor of the sailing ship versus one driven by steam power. For many years shipbuilders continued to follow the design of hull developed for the use of sailing ships, not the most efficient design for power-driven hulls. It took time for designers to work out how a differently designed hull could be more effective. So one of the features reflected back to us is that we need to be accustomed to the use of new technologies so that we can create new learning activities with them, rather than just use the equipment with activities we already know. On the other hand, the younger we are, the better we take to new technologies; after all they are not 'new' to us as we have no memory of what went before and do not have to accommodate our learning to take account of old practices.

'Reflection' shows us also what we already knew, the 'multi-experience' of learners as well as 'multi-ability'. Indeed, perhaps it shows us more clearly that 'multi-experience' is a highly significant factor. I recently observed a classroom in an FE College where the course was entirely based on learning how to use SAGE Accountancy software. I thought teaching this might be an easier prospect than other classes I observed, where students ranged from those with hardly any experience of computers at all to those who were highly developed practitioners, mainly self-taught. All the students on the SAGE course were required to have a basic knowledge of IT skills and clearly were motivated to study this particular package. The trainee was an excellent teacher and after she had introduced the evening's work, I went round and talked with the students. They included single mothers who were desperate to improve their family's financial position and wanted to apply for jobs with a higher salary, an employer who ran a small business and wanted to understand if his accountant was cheating him or not, several people who were self-employed, and a bank manager and other office staff who were using the software daily and wanted to know how to use it in more sophisticated ways. They were all extremely motivated but their purposes in studying the package and their general experience of computer use meant they wanted very different results from the session. Use of ICT brings home to us how singular the individual student is.

Situations where everyone learns from each other (a feature commonly found in ICT usage) takes courage to implement, particularly in classes where the teacher is both disciplinarian as well as learning organiser. The provisional nature of work, such as re-drafting or feeding in new data, takes time to implement. Good practice exists but cannot be universal yet. So, moving on from whichever position we have attained in ICT usage and evaluating our progress are the important factors. Just as children learning to word process alongside learning to write move from stage to stage and the progress itself should be encouraged (Monteith, 1999), similarly so should classroom use of ICT. We need more ICT case studies, such as those given by Tyldesley (2002) and Moseley et al.(1999) preferably with the help of observers and in consultation with pupils and students, so that we can tell what progressive stages there are and how we can implement them in a range of contexts. These case studies would not be in the nature of 'hectoring' good practice or ideal models, but ones we could relate to in terms of our own progress and which we could discuss with others in terms of our own philosophy as regards teaching and learning.

Is one solution: 'Not to worry whose voice is heard in the essay'?

This section considers a model where views of ICT integration are highly advanced. Pickering (1995) suggests we should not worry whose voice is heard and explains:

> ...students could offer their own writing along with other sources composed with images, sounds and annotated links into an interactive hypertextual web. The essay becomes the composition. The problem for the instructor is to gauge the competence or talent of the composer. Instead of the extended critical essay, we have the contrastive linking and ironic juxtaposition of sources which discloses the student's capacity to take a critical stance to the subject.

This is culturally very difficult for us as western educationalists to accept. Usually, we expect to receive a particular piece of writing or other work (whatever subject or age) from an individual and then assess it. The work may be commented on, put up on the wall as a good example or graded for a public examination. As pupils or students we may not like the grades or comments given; as teachers we may not like the effect that assessment has on subjects or on those subjects which are not assessed; but on the whole we believe such a system works. ICT reflects back some of the problems integral to such an assessment system: notably those of collaboration and plagiarism.

Collaboration was deemed to be one of the most useful features of work with ICT when computers were first introduced into schools. In some part, this may have been due to the fact that most schools possessed only one or two computers and therefore collaborative work was an obvious solution in terms of use. Nevertheless, such collaborative work was largely omitted from the 1988 National Curriculum guidelines no doubt owing to assessment anxiety as to who was completing which task on the computer. There are solutions to the assessment dilemma with collaborative or co-operative work (Johnson and Johnson, 1994) and indeed some use of the computer appears to be fundamental now to group work in areas of further and higher education (Monteith and Smith, 2001). Students email each other to arrange meetings; they come together so that they can sit and discuss their project with a computer screen in front of them. They use the computer as an adjunct, a table, drawing space, or tool kit while they focus together on their project. Students certainly believe that working with a computer aids collaboration.

Pupils in school usually need to learn how to work collaboratively. The SLANT project found that when children were placed in groups around a computer, they frequently did not work together well (Mercer, N. 1994). This evidence supports the notion that use of ICT can reflect our normal behaviour, as presumably the same children did not act collaboratively together in group work with or without a computer. So, in one sense, the teacher has to be concerned with whose voices are heard in the work, as some might not be heard at all and others too frequently. With guidance, pupils' collaboration can improve considerably (Wegerif, R. and Dawes,

L.1997). However, as long as assessment of the individual voice remains such an essential component of our educational system, collaborative work will remain difficult to implement fully.

Plagiarism is an even more problematic issue. The work of an individual is paramount in terms of his or her move up the educational ladder, gathering 'educational property' on the way. Other cultures, I believe, view this differently and in their context quoting from some other source without necessarily indicating its origin indicates our approval of the source rather than 'theft'. Pickering's curricular suggestion would suit such an arrangement. Chandler (1989) stated that we have experienced five centuries of print-based technology, which has encouraged us to embrace authorship, copyright and the concept of plagiarism. He predicted that life in a 'networked society' would lead us to reverse these features of print-based technology.

It is likely that the ability to plagiarise easily (there are now plenty of essays and other assessment tasks available on the Internet) may change assessment models. The examination system still stands firm however, and a recent finding that children undertaking examinations are less likely to be involved in work with ICT indicates how teachers believe that sticking to the old methods brings better results. (IMPACT2, 2002)

Conclusion

Educators continue with their own philosophies about teaching and learning if they seem to work. Good practice examples are never entirely successful in bringing about change and can be counterproductive if considered as 'hectoring'. Yet the good practice model is seemingly adopted by teachers as the best one available.

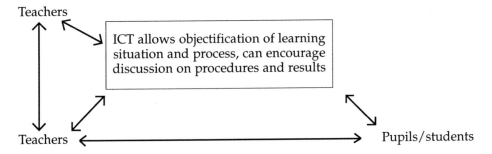

Figure 1: Reflective Capacity of ICT in learning process

Both teachers and pupils are learning. Teachers bring more knowledge of learning to the learning situation, not necessarily expertise in the particular item being studied. Pupils /students bring with them a variety of experience and range of purpose.
Change occurs in learning and teaching when we reflect upon our own responses,

attitudes and philosophy. This is particularly important for us as teachers as otherwise habitual and unrecognised responses will significantly influence our teaching role. It is not enough to show people good examples of the use of ICT, though these might well be useful to those of us who are already in the process of change. We need to be able to recognise where we have reached in terms of ICT usage, to refine our learning models and to go on learning. All educators should be encouraged to create case studies relating to their own experience with ICT and these could be assembled in an organised series to enable us to recognise and reflect upon our own progress.

References

BECTa (2000) *A preliminary report for the DfEE on the relationship between ICT and primary school standards – an analysis of Ofsted inspection data for 1998 – 9*, BECTa: Coventry

Carroll, T. *'If we didn't have the schools we have today – would we create the schools we have today?'* Keynote address: Society for Information Technology and Teacher Education Conference, San Diego California. February 2000

Chandler, D. (1989) Computers and Literacy. In Chandler, D. and Marcus, S. *Computers and Literacy*. Milton Keynes: OU Press

Chesney, M. (2000) 'Beacon Schools'. *Guardian Education*, December 5th 2000 p6

Cordingley, P (2000) 'Teacher Perspectives on the Accessibility and Usability of Research outputs'. BERA Conference. Disseminated by the Teacher Training Agency, London

Higgins, S. and Moseley, M. (2002) 'Raising Achievement in Literacy through ICT'. In Monteith, M. (ed). *Teaching Primary Literacy with ICT*. Open University Press. Milton Keynes

IMPACT 2, Department for Education and Skills, at BECTa website February 2002:www.becta.org.uk

Jarvis, G. (2001) Breaking Down the Barriers of IT. In the *Newsletter of the Association of Information Technology*, 2001. Number 38

Jarvis, G. (2002) Personal email communication to editor

Johnson, D. W., and Johnson, R. T. (1994). *Learning Together and Alone*. Englewood Cliffs, New Jersey: Prentice Hall.

Mercer, N. 'The quality of children's talk in joint activity at the computer'. *Journal of Computer Assisted Learning* 10 (1994): 24-32

Monteith M. (1999) 'Computer Literacy' in Marsh and Hallet (eds) *Desirable Literacies*. Paul Chapman Publishing. London

Monteith, M. and Smith, J. 'Learning in a Virtual Campus: the Pedagogical Implications of Student Experience'. Innovations in Education and Training International (IETI) ed. Barker, P. (2001): 119-132

Moseley D. et al.(1999) *Ways Forward with ICT: Effective Pedagogy using Information and Communications Technology in Literacy and Numeracy in Primary Schools* Newcastle upon Tyne: University of Newcastle upon Tyne, (ISBN 0 7017 0086 6)

Oldknow A. and Taylor R. (1998) *Data-capture and modelling in mathematics and science*. Coventry: BECTa

Owen E. (2000) *Cooperation and Teachers Professional Career Curriculum, Evaluation and*

Promotion. Paper given at the ATEE (Association of Teachers in European Education) Conference. Barcelona

Rodriguez, M. and Ferrante A. (1996) IT for 21st Century. Computational Mechanics Publications

Pickering J.(1995) Teaching on the Internet is Learning, Active Learning 2

Tomlinson, M. as quoted: TES Online, 9 March 2001

Turkle, S. (1984) *The Second Self: Computers and the Human Spirit*. Simon and Schuster. New York

Tyldesley, A. (2002) A reflective view of the English National Literacy Strategy. In Monteith (ed.) *Teaching Primary Literacy*. Milton Keynes. Open University Press

Wegerif R. and Dawes L. (1997) 'Computers and Exploratory Talk: an intervention study'. In Wegerif R. and Scrimshaw P. (eds) *Computers and Talk in the Primary Classroom*. Multi-lingual Matters: Clevedon, 1997

Yazdani Masoud (1987) *New Horizons in Educational Computing*. Chichester, England. Ellis Horwood Limited

Just a Tool? The Computer as the Curriculum

Martin Owen

This chapter proceeds from the notion that curriculum is not something that is a given or obvious but is socially determined by culture and history in both manifest and subtle ways. As culture is determined by our language and the tools we use, the development of new communicative capacity will radically change our culture. The ubiquity of information technologies will be a strong determinant in what the curriculum will be. Indeed, the existence of the computer will change the way we think and learn as well as what we learn and think. I challenge a remark I often hear: 'the computer is just a tool', where just and tool are meant to indicate that effects are minimal, as though the computer is benign or has a level of importance akin to a trouser press.

I do not take a simplistic *technologically deterministic* view, ascribing the nature of our social being to the technologies we have discovered, nor do I want to state an opposing view that *'Shakespeare would not have written different/better plays if he had had a word processor'*. Rather, I argue in support of Bijker (1987) who suggests there is a rich and seamless web between our society and the technologies we use, and that in turn influences what we are, how we see the world, what we talk about, what we do. I shall refer to models of learning and being, which are described by socio-cultural psychology , based on the work of Vygotsky (1978) and Leont'ev (1978) to help explain how new cultural artefacts lead to different ways of being in the world. I also draw on the work of Bateson (1972) on change of learning and speculate on ways we can think differently about what and how we teach now.

Technology and Society, a Seamless Web

The tools we make and inherit are shaped by us and in turn the tools shape the way we are in the world. When the Wright brothers took to the air it was not with the motive that northern Europeans could eat asparagus at Christmas. Yet the logistics of bringing fresh asparagus from Peru to northwest Wales are founded on their engineering feat. The aeroplane provides a mode of shopping that allows shops in relatively rural north Wales to carry thousands of different foods in twenty-four-hour-a-day stores. Peruvian villages have new opportunities in terms of how a 'living' is made. Producing exotic vegetables for a northern market changes ways of life. The political geography and village architecture change. Peruvians have new questions they can ask because new activities and life choices come into being. Of course other technologies (e.g. highways, refrigeration etc.) have parts to play but the aeroplane *tool* has fundamentally changed perception and action in the world. What counts as an *appropriate* education for a Peruvian villager may have changed radically.

Changes in the Peruvian way of life were not determined by the aeroplane. Nor are/were they predictable. However, the aeroplane has mediated the activity of people in those villages so that what they think and do is in part formed by its existence. It is hard to speculate on the consequences for whole ways of life in the *information age*. What we might perceive as normal courses of action in the future are not readily available to us at present. We might speculate as to the mechanisms whereby changes might take place (for we are still the same biological organism). We can examine and evaluate what is happening around us at present: the emergent patterns of change in activity and the social context in which we operate. In passing there are two not coincidental facts. The world's first commercial computer[1] was made in the UK for the logistics of the food industry (Lyons). Secondly, the first computer in my home town was for the headquarters of one of the first UK supermarket chains.

Style and clarity of handwriting formed highly significant parts of the curriculum until relatively recently. Much school time was devoted to learning to write in specific clear styles relating to copperplate writing. The user of the fountain pen had major advantages in having clear, continuous and blot free text and was thus ideally suited to the production of *copperplate* writing. Handwriting was the technology of business communication and recording–a significant factor in employability. 'Copperplate' style was not just the preferred style for business but also had its origins in earlier technology; its name derives from a writing style used on copper plates for etching. This needed a writing style that minimised the need to lift the stylus off the plate. A number of technological issues acted together to determine what was a critical curriculum activity in schools. The move to typewriters and, subsequently, the computer changed curriculum requirements.

My last example of the nature of change in thinking that comes with tool development poses questions about information carried on paper. How does a simple information retrieval act vary (in its planning and execution) in the following technological configuration of paper-based information management?

a) a pile of papers apparently randomly arranged in a heap on a desk

b) paper arranged in books with titles on their spine apparently randomly arranged in a heap on a desk

c) paper arranged in books with titles on their spine placed randomly on shelving

d) paper arranged in books with titles on their spine placed in order according to their owner's personal classification system

e) paper arranged in books with titles on their spine placed in order according to a standard classification system

f) paper arranged in books with titles on their spine placed in order according to a standard classification system, where the books have been indexed and have contents pages.

And so on….

What is possible and what we think is possible changes with the application of these technologies. Changing the technology causes us to think differently about what we can know from books, and what we teach from paper is mediated by the technologies and systems we have devised for the construction and storage of printed media.

These examples indicate that the context in which we act and the tools we use influence the way we act in the world. The use of tools and cultural artefacts forms the basis of understanding the process of thinking and learning as initially described by Vygotsky, and may help to explain why and what information technology may do to change thinking and learning.

Activity Theory and Learning

The following ideas provide a basis for understanding the cultural and historic contexts which we (as learners) are in, the role of computer tools in society and their capability as tools for transformation and empowerment. Activity theory comes from the work of Vygotsky and was developed by Leont'ev; it proposes the idea that tools mediate thought. Vygotsky's work showed that the mind emerges through interaction with the environment. Our mental practices develop and emerge through a process of internalisation of external activity. Tools and/or cultural artefacts are the mediation system: instruments, signs, language, procedures, machines, laws, methods, and forms of work organisation, rituals and accepted practices. In turn humans develop more tools and cultural artefacts.

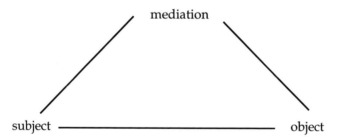

Figure 1: The triangular representation of mediation

If you, the subject, need to act on some object or goal, the process of action is determined by your past learning, your historical and cultural situation and the tools that are to hand. Wertsch (1998) describes the way in which pole vaulting as an activity changes when you move from wood to aluminium to composite fibre material. The vaulter's apparently autonomous kinetic gestures are significantly different yet the goal is the same. Changing the mediation system changes the activity.

The process of mediation provides a basis for my argument that use of information technology will fundamentally change the way we think and learn and thus change education and the curriculum. I stress, however, that this is not deterministic. Technology does not act alone and outcomes are all uncertain. The whole panoply of tools and cultural artefacts acts together to determine the shape of education. The outcome will vary from context to context.

Following Vygotsky, Engeström and Cole (1993) suggest that for an activity to be fully understood we must understand how artefacts mediate the activity within the totality of a cultural context. Engeström and Cole elaborate a wider set of relationships to describe an activity (figure 2).

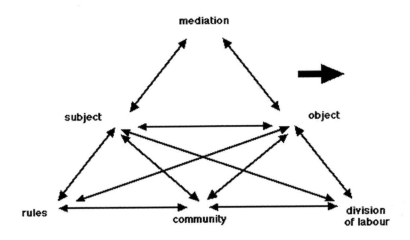

Figure 2: From Engeström and Cole (1983)

In their analysis, the individual (the subject of the activity) and the individual's goal or purpose (the object of the activity) are mediated by tools and symbol systems are extended in a particular way. They show that subjects are not isolated in a system but behave in ways determined by their membership of and participation in that community. Further, the full range of that community's tools mediates the subject's activity within the community. In turn the community's relationship to the object is determined by the division of labour and resources within the community. That is to say each member of a community plays a role in an activity. That role may be determined by the power and responsibility they possess, their access to and capability with mediation. Clearly rules and regulations external to the system will also have major influences.

In summary, Cole and Engeström see that individuals participating in an activity leading to some goal will be affected by the following factors:
- the tools used (instruments, signs and language)
- the community the individual belongs to (values, hierarchies, rituals, rules and accepted practices)
- the division of labour in that community (roles, responsibilities, co-ordination and communication procedures)

In turn these are not unidirectional. The tools, mediation system, rules of the community and division of labour affect the mental processes that develop for each individual.

From this application of Activity Theory it is possible to hypothesize about the ways that information technologies will profoundly influence the education system. The introduction of new artefacts into an activity changes what happens within the activity, both socially and for the individual. Similarly, existing practices and processes of the community in which the activity takes place and the mental processes of individuals doing the activity affect how a new artefact will be used. New tools and processes make changes throughout the system and changes within the system change how an artefact is used.

Learning and Context

Contrary to the arguments I present there are authorities who feel that there are eternal verities. There is a belief in the idea of distinctive subjects that have their own philosophical validity. This strong philosophical current can be seen in the selection of subjects of the National Curricula in England and Wales since 1988 (Phenix, P. 1969, Hirst, P. H. 1975). The subjects chosen for the 2000s would not seem unfamiliar to the Grammar School or Public School of the 1900s. Motor vehicle mechanics, computer studies, and film and TV studies are not in the National Curriculum. The idea of a 'proper' curriculum of 'essential, 'eternally valuable knowledge' is a powerful current with influential supporters.

This chapter goes further than just suggesting that technology changes the curriculum. I suggest that learning itself changes. This argument requires careful attention to the role of the context in which learning takes place. Gregory Bateson proposed a framework for understanding learning with a basis founded on human action as a human organism within an ecosystem. Bateson was concerned to define the mind in terms of mindful action in relation to the mind's context. The central theme of his argument is that there are levels of nesting learning strategy that should be distinguished and that each level has properties not predictable from the one before. Each strategy, therefore, gives rise to a unique learning type. These are described as Learning I, II and III etc.

In *zero learning* an entity shows minimum change in its response to minimum sensory input. These are the kinds of habituated actions. We feel pain, hunger and so on. The word 'learn' is often applied to what is here called 'zero learning': for example, I 'learn' from the school bell that it is twelve o'clock. It does not allow for change by trial and error. Bateson attaches great importance to this. Trial and error give rise to the possibility of learning becoming a process of creative adjustment, in what Bateson describes as a stochastic environment. This is where a sequence of events combines a random component with a selective process so that only certain outcomes of the random are allowed to endure. It allows a set of increasingly sophisticated corrective strategies.

Learning I implies that at one time the entity is in one state and at another time in the future the entity is in another state as a result of some process. This is often what is described as learning in psychology laboratories (see the works of Skinner B. F. 1979).

Figure 3: Learning 1 is characterised by a new behaviour in the same context

Bateson makes an important point about context in learning:

> Note that in all cases of Learning I, there is in our description an assumption about "context." This assumption must be made explicit. The definition of Learning I assumes that the buzzer (the stimulus) is somehow the "same" at Time 1 and Time 2. And this assumption of "sameness" must also delimit the "context," which must (theoretically) be the same at both times. It follows that the events which occurred at Time 1 are not, in our description, included in our definition of the context at Time 2, because to include them would at once create a gross difference between "context at Time 1" and "context at Time 2".
>
> (Bateson, 1979:293)

Context here is a collective term for all those events that tell the organism among what set of alternatives he must make his next choice. An organism responds to the 'same' stimulus differently in differing contexts, and we must therefore ask about the source of the organism's information. From what percept does he know that Context A is different from Context B?

The next stage of complexity, with a capacity for correction, is that difference itself has to make a difference. This can only occur where there are consistent boundaries, or 'a context'. The degree of change between Zero Learning and Learning I is a distinctive step from first difference and then context. Therefore, Learning II, the next stage in the progression of sophistication of corrective strategies demands an awareness of pattern.

Learning II is probably best characterised by learning to learn. This is the ability to see a new learning context as similar to one that has been experienced before and then be able to remember and transfer skills that were found to be appropriate for that previous context into the new one. Learning II is a high-order phenomenon involving pattern recognition and applying templates. As context changes so does the appropriateness of a response to a given stimulus.

Learning 2

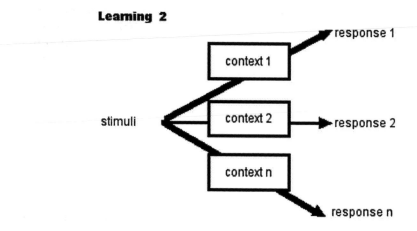

Figure 4: Response to stimuli is varied according to experiences in different contexts

Learning III is change in the process of Learning II, a corrective change in the system of sets of alternatives from which choice is made. It is the process of learning how we manage our learning, to see ways of moving beyond what we already know, managing the contexts, the ability to change our learning strategies. Thus when we encounter and resolve contradictions amongst contexts we formulate new contexts.

The most significant factor in this 'learning' is the issue of context and changing contexts. At level 1, the response to a stimulus changes with the context; the next level (2) gives us a degree of choice of behaviour in specific contexts and further next level (3) is about changing management and changing contexts and so on.

Learning 3

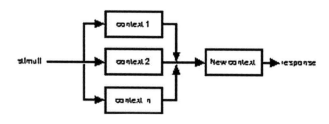

Figure 5: The corrective change in our understanding of contexts

We are in a changing context now. If I walked through woodland as a gamekeeper I would see and think different things to a townsperson. The contexts in which my 'knowing' was gained determine what I find 'thinkable'. This relates directly back to the earlier discussion about how we organise knowledge on paper. What knowledge can be gained, how it is feasible to come to know changes with the techno-cultural organisation of knowledge. The culture in which you come to know is an important feature of how and what you know. The context of the digital age provides new tools for seeing, finding, interacting, communicating, envisioning, enacting, pattern forming, empathising. Dealing with the world is mediated through a different set of cultural artefacts. This is not *just a tool*. This is a time of Level 3 change.

How big is the IT contextual change?

This question is at the heart of the digital literacy issue. One solution is to believe the computer is *just a tool*. One can teach and undertake courses in the use of various computer applications: word processing, spreadsheets, web surfing and so on. The operation and mechanics of these tools seem to form the core of a number of key qualifications. The mechanics of specific computer applications seem to form the basis of secondary school examinations like GCSE (General Certificate of Education), CoE (Certificate of Education), the ECDL (European Computer driving Licence) or CLAIT (Computer Literacy and Information Technology). Examining the tasks set in 2001for 16 + (Curriculum 2000) key skills in information technology it appears that the ability to perform a mail merge between a word processor and a relational database management system from the same software company is a *key skill*, a new curricular idea that some "skills" are key to all other knowing.

The metaphor of the driving licence is interesting. If a box can be ticked indicating that a person can mix text and graphics in a document, or can add up a list of numbers in a spreadsheet, that qualifies one as being 'computer literate'. It tells you nothing about the ways that the aesthetics or semiotics of your communication methods are developing, neither does it tell you about the ways in which you may now envision quantity or relationship. Taking the driving licence further, the ability to change gear is not the major life issue arising from automobile technology. Living in suburbs, the separation of workplace from dwelling and all the ways that changes our way of life, are more significant in *learning* about living our lives with automobiles.

Clearly undertaking this kind of activity in schools and colleges give students something to do in information technology. The software is often provided free alongside the hardware. The activities are tractable and require only a little planning by anybody modestly competent in the use of the software. They do not disrupt the rest of the curriculum. Even though information technology in this context is labelled a *key skill* it can happily exist in its own space.

It seems to be the software that is commonly used in commerce. This, in a sense, gives an authenticity to the activities. It is easy to conceive of activities such as spreadsheets for soft drinks concessions at youth centres. However, as a solution to a perceived *computer literacy* or *digital literacy* problem it is deeply flawed. It considers a narrow spectrum of potential computer use and fails to examine the ways the processes themselves change the ways that working and learning can happen. Aspects of using these tools that are deeply relevant for their application in the real world are missing. In developing models with the spreadsheet the very process of modelling *per se* receives little prominence; in creating a document with text and graphics, what makes an effective communication is ignored.

Previous criticisms of 'computer literacy' tend to focus on its technicist nature. In particular Webster and Robins (1991) identify major problems in teaching about technology in isolation. This is strongly echoed by Beynon (1993):

> Too many courses still start with technology rather than with education and force educational concerns too readily into the computer format rather than identifying the educational goals and ensuring that the technology is appropriate (or adapted) to serve these... The 'How?' associated with skills training must be always be secondary to the 'Why?' associated with technological literacy.

Analysis

JITTE Vol 2 No 1

Whereas I sympathise with this position, I would contend it is not too easy to separate the 'how' from the 'why'. Too much reliance on 'why' places the learner in the role of the critic rather than the performer. There is an assumed primacy of the educational and the cultural over the technical which I cannot separate so easily.

Robins and Webster (1999) have a long history of criticism of technicist computer literacy and their thesis links digital literacy with organisational relationships with capitalism that echoes earlier analyses of curriculum, schooling and power from writers like Bowles and Gintis (1975). Robins and Webster believe that education systems have the capacity to adjust effectively to new economic systems and following Foucault, knowledge is intimately connected to power. Therefore the models of digital literacy we are developing are extensions to a system of social control and what they term as neoFordism in the workplace and in educational institutions.

They see the 'Hallmark of Neo-Fordism is its flexibility (decentralized, fragmented, disseminated), manifested in changed forms of production and patterns of consumption, and class relations which are characterized by increasing individuation and differentiation, though with particularly marked divisions between core and peripheral workers' (1999:170).

- At school level, education is becoming more centralized and local autonomy has been reduced
- Flexibility is an objective; more teaching of competencies and skills rather than traditional subjects; experiential, project-based, and problem-solving pedagogy rather than didactic academic methods; emphasis on technology and computer literacy, etc.
- We are witnessing *neo-Fordist* education produce an adaptable, flexible, integrated workplace.

Digital literacy is seen as a key component in this process, and cybernetic models of social control pervade learning, learning systems and information technology in general. The computer tools we implement therefore have characteristics that are best fitted to the ways that suit global capitalism:

- Cybernetic theory interprets social, psychological, and biological processes in terms of feedback loops and control loops
- It is not neutral, it privileges mechanic over holistic thinking; cognition over intuition, calculative over deliberate life.

Using computer tools as they are currently conceived induces more 'capitalist' friendly modes of action. Robins and Webster refer to such a process as *Instrumental Progressivism* and identify currents in education and educational computing that map on to this concept.

In relation to Computer Literacy they note that:

- Paperts's *Mindstorms* (1981), one of the most successful cognitivist positions in describing education with and about computers, includes as a salient factor that LOGO and LOGO-like activities assimilate human psychic processes to those of the computer and that is a characteristic of instrumental progressivism
- that the computer is deeply implicated in the transformation of our self-image and in relations of power and control;
- that this is not a by-product but an intrinsic and constitutive aspect central to evolving 'progressive' social control.

They note there is a transformation from what they term Mode 1 knowledge (homogeneous, rooted in a strong academic and hierarchically organized, apprentice-master relationship) to Mode 2 knowledge (non-hierarchical, pluralistic, trans-disciplinary, fast changing, responsive to students' experiences, industrial priorities, and social problems). I can readily identify that the kinds of digital literacy I support would tend to produce such a transition. Clearly, Mode1 knowledge dates from an earlier formation of capitalist production where the need for academic elites, and the support of a dilettanté class were functions of universities and major parts of the education system. It is not clear from reading Robins and Webster what might be a more appropriate form of computer literacy. Obviously, a critical stance as suggested by Beynon needs to be taken, however this will inevitably bring learners into contact with tools developed within a neoFordist environment. I suggest elsewhere (Owen 1999) that there is a need for tools developed by the education community for the education community. However, this would still be problematic in Robins and Webster's terms because the educational thinking which would inform their design is still based in neoFordist thinking.

Robins and Webster firmly set their understanding of the role of computers and learning in a full cultural and historic setting, with an appreciation that information technology and its applications change education and what needs to be known. Robins and Webster are concerned that we should not accept this position uncritically: we should be aware that there are economic and political choices to be made. This can be understood by using the cultural-historic activity framework proposed by Engeström and described above.

Rozak(1999) takes a different point of view. He states bluntly:

> Lesson No. 1 in computer literacy is that the computer contributes nothing essential to the life of the mind.....Shakespeare never lost a document to a computer crash.
>
> *New York Times*, 11 March 1999

It is perhaps easy to dispose of an argument hinged on the word 'essential' as in biological terms very few available cultural artefacts are *essential* to the life of the mind.

Rozak's main contentions are that the computer adds nothing new and in spending time on the computer we are detracting from that which is more useful. He dismisses the Internet as a marketing man's dream tool. However, marketing men have also used all other media that preceded the computer: print, drama, visual arts or whatever. Rozak is fond of saying money spent on computers in schools should be spent on public libraries. No one has sought to limit access to books on the basis that printed material is also used for advertising .

Another of Rozak's criticisms (1986) is that information technology has spawned an information overload: 'An excess of information may actually crowd out ideas, leaving the mind (young minds especially) distracted by sterile, disconnected facts, lost among shapeless heaps of data'.

One is tempted to say the easiest way to deal with complexity of information is to remain illiterate. Rozak forms part of the tradition that holds there are some forms of knowledge superior to others, in a sense re-affirming the tradition of positivist philosophy from Hirst and Phenix. There is a continuing assumption of an inviolable, unchanging bedrock culture which must be accessed in order to be *educated*. However, the world is increasing in complexity and Rozaks's reading of the relationship between technology, society and education goes against history.

Critical Digital Literacy

Education, according to Freire, is for the purpose of humanizing others through conscious action for the purposes of transforming the world. Freire and his co-workers were opposed to teaching merely the instrumental and decontextualized skills of reading and writing. They preferred to present participation in the political process through knowledge of reading and writing as a desirable and attainable goal for all Brazilians. Freire won the attention of the poor and awakened their hope that they could start to have a say in the day-to-day decisions that affected their lives. This *liberatory education* encourages learners to challenge and change the world, not merely uncritically adapt themselves to it. The content and purpose of liberatory education is the collective responsibility of learners, teachers, and the community alike who, through dialogue, seek political, as well as economic and personal empowerment.

Freire stated: Technology is nothing more or less than a natural phase of the creative process which engaged man from the moment he forged his first tool and began to transform the world for its humanization.' (Freire, 1974) There is herein a belief that technology is a human system. The pedagogy Freire suggested as a means to empowerment is described as *Praxis*, a complex activity by which individuals create culture and society, and become critically conscious human beings. Praxis comprises a cycle of action-reflection-action that is central to liberatory education. Characteristics of praxis include self-determination (as opposed to coercion), intentionality (as opposed to reaction), creativity (as opposed to homogeneity), and rationality (as opposed to chance). This not only demands the acquisition of skills but also the putting of skills into operation for self- and community-inspired transformation.

So what is a digital curriculum?

There can be no fixed rules for we are in a state of transformation, we have different needs and exist in different cultural, historical and technological circumstances. Our contexts are constantly changing. There are elements within the development and application of technology that can readily be developed as part of our empowerment. Fortunately in England and Wales some of these elements are recognised in the National Curriculum. Within the framework of activity this is a clear advantage. It offers many possibilities for excellent transformational practice. Some examples of mandated activity for students include:

- how to analyse the requirements of tasks, taking into account the information they need and the ways they will use it
- discriminate in their use of information sources and ICT tools
- use ICT effectively to explore, develop and interpret information and solve problems in a variety of subjects and contexts
- apply, as appropriate, the concepts and techniques of ICT-based modelling, considering their advantages and limitations against other methods
- use information sources and ICT tools effectively to share, exchange and present information in a variety of subjects and contexts
- reflect critically on the impact of ICT on their own and others' lives, considering the social, economic, political, legal, ethical and moral issues.

(http://www.nc.uk.net/servlets/Subjects?Subject=ICT)

These have enormous potential as objectives for transformation. However, if we examine the suggested schemes of work (http://www.standards.dfee.gov.uk/schemes2/secondary_ICT/ict04/?version=1) there is a slide into unimaginative casting of modelling as running a small retail enterprise like a 'tuck-shop'. Modelling and financial control using a spreadsheet makes the transformational power of the computer into a low-grade clerical task. Multimedia communication becomes a mechanical process of mixing text and graphical items with little critical inspection. The technology is given pre-eminence over the information in National Curriculum IT lessons I visit.

Learners can be empowered to create electronic documents and communication as never before; however, they need to have a critical understanding of the power of that communication. They need education in the semiotics and aesthetics of the communication systems they are using. The technological capability of mixing a digital photograph with some text is trivial. Knowing the power of the juxtaposition of the right text and the right digital photograph is the substance of a transformative education. That we are able to extend this power to learners is a gift of information technologies and needs embedding in a praxi-based curriculum.

Modelling is more than retail outlets and spreadsheets. The computer was developed as a modelling tool. How many different ways are there of representing information as a dynamic model in a computer? Are some ways better than others? Do some methods lend themselves to the representation of some problems better than others? Are there systems limitations apparent to the interpreter? Does the representation of the information provide multiple viewpoints of that information? Do users know what are good ways of envisioning information? How do you come to know this stuff? What should the curriculum be? Herein lie some tensions that are alluded to in considering the activity system of teaching IT in present-day schools. There are clear contradictions that need illuminating and amplifying.

A computer curriculum can lead to active learning that engages students in making their own meanings and understanding of the contexts they are in. Of course at the centre is human interaction. The computer is a mediating tool. Human interaction is an important factor in learning, and sharing ideas and collaborating are essential components of learning and further professional development. Praxis learning is at its best when it is task based, and when students and professionals are engaged in a reflective exploration of an authentic task which builds new skills, knowledge and understanding for the student or professional. Garbinger and Dunlap (1995) define a 'Rich Environment for Active Learning' (REALS) as the basis for a comprehensive instructional system which evolves from and is consistent with constructivist philosophies and theories, a system which:

- promotes study and investigation within authentic contexts
- encourages the growth of student responsibility, initiative decision making, and intentional learning
- cultivates collaboration amongst students and teachers
- utilises dynamic, interdisciplinary, generative learning activities that promote higher-order thinking processes to help students develop rich and complex knowledge structures
- assesses student progress in content and learning-to-learn within authentic contexts using realistic tasks and performances.

A curriculum should also address the argument advanced by Kinchloe and Steinberg (1993) that modern analysis of our world understanding needs to establish cognitive theories that transcend deterministic Newtonian-Cartesian certainties. Kinchloe and Steinberg postulate a need for post-formal thinking (in the Piagetian sense). The features of a curriculum that cultivate this thinking are:

- *etymology* - the exploration of the forces that produce what the culture validates as knowledge
- *pattern* - the understanding of the connecting patterns and relationships that undergird the lived world
- *process* - the cultivation of new ways to read the world that attempt to make sense of both ourselves and contemporary society
- *contextualisation* - the appreciation that knowledge can never stand alone or be complete in and of itself.

Here is a vision of a curriculum in which there is an acceptance of uncertainty in the world, certainly true for a curriculum which has to address questions such as: 'How do I deal with other people?' It leads to the need for learning support that allows choice, a range of potential solutions and problems to be presented, with each problem examined from a variety of contrasting view points; collaborative teaching and learning. It is also a curriculum where learners can be empowered by digital tools.

The Computer as Curriculum

'When we create new tools we create new conversations'.

Understanding Computers and Cognition (Winograd and Flores)

It is difficult to get outside ourselves and see culture changes the way a historian can. The pattern of our history is hard to read at the time it is being written. Our contexts are surely changing in a radical manner. The changes in context may need highly critical scrutiny as observers like Robins and Webster suggest. Our modes of action in the world will change, and digital technologies are a significant factor in that change. Their use and application will be a significant mediation system in our thinking, what and how we learn should therefore follow this change in context. It will probably be better if this happens deliberately rather than accidentally.

If we are stuck with a curriculum which was designed for another age, with other tools and other contexts clear contradictions will emerge. These may have unforeseen social consequences which are beyond the scope of this chapter. However, it is time educational reformers ceased tinkering with adjustments to the old curriculum and start to consider what is emerging from our new contexts. ▪

References

Bijker, W. et al. (1987) The social construction of technological systems. new directions in the sociology and history of technology. Cambridge, Mass.. London. MIT Press. 1987

Bateson G., and Bateson M.C. (1972) Steps to the Ecology of Mind. Balantine, New York

Beynon, J. (1993)'Technological Literacy: where do we go from here?', Journal of Information Technology in Education, 2 (1)7-36

Bowles, S. and Gintis H. (1976) *Schooling in Capitalist America*. New York: Basic Books Inc.

Engeström, Y. & Cole, M. (1993). A cultural-historical approach to distributed cognition. In Soloman, G. (Ed.) *Distributed Cognition*, Cambridge: Cambridge University Press, 1-46

Freire P. (1974) "Cultural Action for Freedom" Penguin, Harmondsworth

Grabinger, R. S. & Dunlap, J. (1995). Rich Environments for active learning. *Alt-J*, 3 (2), 5-34

Hirst, P. H. (1975). Liberal education and the nature of knowledge. In R. F. Deardon, P. H. Hirst, & R. S. Peters (Eds.), Education & reason (pp. 1-24). London: Routledge & Kegan Paul

Kinchloe, J. L. & Steinberg, S. R. (1993). A tentative Description of Post-Formal Thinking: The Critical Confrontation with Cognitive theory. *Harvard Educational Review*, 63 (3), 296-319

Leont'ev, A. N. (1978). *Activity, consciousness, and personality*, Englewood Cliffs: Prentice-Hall

Owen, M. (1999) 'Appropriate and appropriated technology: technological literacy and educational software standards'. *Educational Technology & Society* 2(4) 1999 ISSN 1436-4522

Papert, S. (1981) *Mindstorms*, Harvester Press, Brighton

Phenix, P. H. (1969). The use of the disciplines as curriculum content. In D. Vandenberg (Ed.), Theory of knowledge and problems of education. Urbana, IL: University of Illinois Press

Rozak, Theodore (1986). The cult of information: the folklore of computers and the true art of thinking. Pantheon, 1986

Skinner, B. F,(1976) "About behaviorism " B. F. Skinner New York: Vintage Books, 1976

Vygotsky, L. S. (1978). *Mind in society: The development of higher psychological processes*, Edited by M. Cole, V. J. Steiner, S. Scribner & E. Souberman, Cambridge, MA: Harvard University Press

Webster, F. & Robins, K. (1991) The selling of the new technology, in Mackay, H., Young, M.F.D. & Beynon, J. (Eds) Falmer, Brighton

Webster F. and Robins K. (1999) The technical fix: education, computers and industry. Basingstoke: Macmillan, 1999

Wertsch, J. (1998). Mind as action. New York: Oxford University Press

Winograd T., (1986) Flores, F. *Understanding Computers and Cognition*. Reading, Mass: Addison-Weseley

---

[i]Leo 1.

First commercial computer, made by Lyons, derived from EDSAC.

In July 47 Lyons made an agreement, giving 3000 pounds and a technician for a year named Lenaerts in exchange for using the EDSACexperience to make their commercial computer called LEO, Lyons Electronic Office. Test programs Feb 15 51, First job 5th Sept 51, dependence complete for one job Nov 30 51.

see Leo : The first business computer. by Peter J. Bird. Hasler Publishing Ltd. 1994

The Computer Practice Framework: a tool to enhance curriculum development relating to ICT

Peter Twining

Introduction

['There has always been a belief, increasingly supported by evidence, that computers can enrich the process of education.']

(McFarlane, 1997:8)

There has been a massive drive to increase the use of information and communications technology (ICT) in education. This is true across different countries within the so-called 'developed world' and different sectors, ranging from primary through higher education and 'life long' learning.

This technology push has been fuelled by a growing number of reports highlighting the importance of ICT to education (Stevenson, Anderson et al. (1997) & Dearing (1997) in the UK; Kerrey, Isakson et al. (2000) in the USA).

> The question is no longer *if* the Internet can be used to transform learning in new and powerful ways. The Commission has found that it can. Nor is the question *should* we invest the time, the energy, and the money necessary to fulfill its promise in defining and shaping new learning opportunity. The Commission believes that we should.

(Kerrey, Isakson et al. 2000:vi)

The overt message within these reports is that we need to harness the potential of ICT to enhance learning. The underlying message is that although ICT has the potential to significantly enhance education that potential is not being realised in practice. This 'reality-rhetoric gap' (Trend, Davis et al. 1999) is widely reflected in the research literature (OFSTED 1997; Underwood and Monteith 1998; Galton, Hargreaves et al. 1999; Moseley, Higgins et al. 1999; OFSTED 1999; DfEE 2000; Preston, Cox et al. 2000). It is further emphasised by continuing calls for additional funding (e.g. Kerrey, Isakson et al. 2000) for ICT in education and by on-going claims that the situation is about to improve:

The year 2000 marks, in effect, the beginning of a new era for IT in FE[i].

(Jameson 2000:2)

This is a depressing picture: despite substantial evidence of the potential of ICT to enhance learning and significant investment in ICT within education it appears to have had relatively little impact. However, those funding education cannot afford to continue to spend such huge sums of money unless they are going to lead to significant enhancements in education.

This lack of impact of ICT investment is partly due to confusion about why we use ICT in education. This leads to muddled thinking about how best to use it. For example, whilst much of the literature on the potential of ICT in education argues that using ICT should transform the curriculum (Trilling and Hood 2001), in practice: 'The Curriculum essentially remains unchanged ... Teachers are being encouraged to teach old knowledge with new technologies' (Cloke 2000:1-2).

I have argued the need to

identify explicit visions of why we want to use ICT and the impact that we want it to have, as well as how we are going to implement those visions in the light of constraints operating in our individual school contexts.

(Twining, 2001a:16)

Three key questions, based on the Computer Practice Framework (CPF) can support the process of developing such visions:
- What are our main objectives for using ICT? (Focus)
- What impact do we want ICT use to have on learning in our institution? (Mode)
- How much time do we want our learners to spend using computers? (Quantity)
  Adapted from Twining (2001a:11)

Our responses to these questions can inform our curriculum development processes and by so doing enhance the effectiveness of investment in 'educational ICT'. Linking the CPF with curriculum development forces us to think more clearly about our use of ICT in education. This, in turn, increases both the impact of our expenditure on ICT and the likelihood we shall achieve our educational goals.

The Curriculum Development Process and The Planning Cycle

Curriculum development is about turning our visions into reality. Our vision, setting out our aspirations, needs to be translated into a plan, what we intend to do given the constraints of our present situation. This is particularly important in the context of ICT because there is often a mismatch between visions of the potential of new technologies to enhance learning and what can realistically be achieved in any particular context. Subsequently, we must implement our plans. We know, both from personal experience and research (Underwood 1988), that there is often a mismatch between what we intend will be learnt and the learning that actually takes place. It is important to assess what is achieved and compare that with our original intentions. This evaluation can then feed back into the planning cycle.

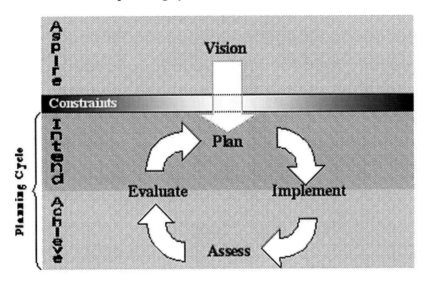

Figure 1: A diagrammatic representation of the stages in a curriculum development process

The curriculum development process, illustrated in figure 1, includes a planning cycle consisting of four consecutive stages. This is an oversimplification: 'in reality each stage is not discrete; you may begin at any point in the cycle and you will not always follow through the whole cycle in order' (Twining and Richards 1999:13). Nevertheless, this model helps us think more clearly about our educational practice. It highlights distinctions between our aspirations (what we would like to do in an ideal world), our intentions (what we plan to do given the constraints within which we have to operate) and what is actually achieved. The Implement stage bridges our intentions with what is achieved, whilst the Evaluate stage allows us to compare the two and thus helps us refine our plans for future action.

The planning cycle operates at a variety of levels.

Level of operation	Stage in planning cycle			
	Plan	**Implement**	**Assess**	**Evaluate**
Long term Whole School	Schemes of work	Management across school	Assessment and recording systems	Review across school
Medium term Key Stage or year group	Term or half-term plans; subjects/topics	Management within team	Co-ordination assessment and recording	Review within team
Short term Class	Lesson plans	Management within class	Assessment	Review of own teaching

Figure 2: The inter-relationship between the stages of the planning cycle and levels at which they can operate within a primary school (Adapted from Twining and Richards 1999:13)

In this chapter, examples come mainly from the context of primary education. For example, figure 2 refers specifically to the planning cycle in a primary school. However, there are direct parallels across the phases: whilst the terminology and examples used within different phases of education vary the underlying processes of curriculum development appear to be the same (as illustrated in figure 3 in relation to the 'Plan' stage of the cycle). Therefore the issues are equally relevant across contexts.

Level of operation Phase	School	**Higher Education Institute**
Long term	Schemes of work	Programme specification
Medium term	Term or half-term plans; subjects/topics	Course specification
Short term	Lesson plans	Lecture plan / session plan

Figure 3: Comparison of terminology used in HE and schools in 'Plan' stage of planning cycle

The Computer Practice Framework (CPF)

This framework describes the 'educational practice' surrounding computer use in education. I began its development in the mid 1990s because I had difficulties in making sense of existing research about computer use in schools. There was much confusion about what people meant by the term 'computer use' which featured extensively within research literature but was often taken to mean very different things

(Twining 1995). Examples ranged from talking about computers without actually using them (Anderson, Hansen et al. 1979) to using them as an integral tool to support learning across the curriculum (Blease and Cohen 1990). Worse still, much research used terms relating to computer use without defining their meaning at all. Before identifying the factors that lead to changes in computer use we need to identify that some changes have taken place; that means we need to be able to describe clearly the ways in which computers are being used.

I set out to find better ways of describing computer use in primary schools. Despite the existence of many frameworks for evaluating software and computer use in schools all of them suffered from significant problems (Twining, 2001b). I therefore carried out a number of exploratory case studies and developed the original version of the CPF. Subsequently the CPF was significantly enhanced as a result of research into its application across a range of different educational contexts. These span primary to HE sectors (Twining 2000b).

The CPF consists of three core dimensions:
- *Quantity*: the quantity of computer use (as a proportion of the available learning time).
- *Focus*: the objectives supported by the computer use.
- *Mode*: the impact of computer use on the curriculum (where curriculum is used in its broadest sense).

These dimensions and sub-divisions are illustrated in figure 4. The framework should be seen holistically – no one dimension on its own provides a sufficiently rich picture.

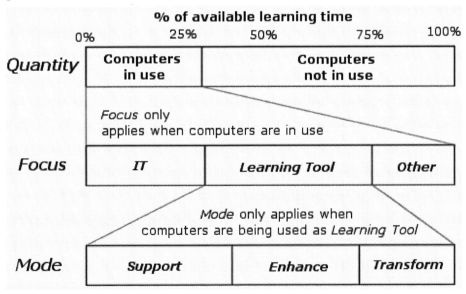

Figure 4: The three dimensions of the CPF

The *Quantity* dimension

This is concerned with the proportion of the school day (available learning time) during which one or more computers are in use by children[ii].

The *Focus* dimension

The Focus deals with the objectives underlying computer use and is sub-divided into three categories:

IT is where your objective is to help the children to develop their IT skills, knowledge and understanding. IT is used here to refer to learning about the technology. The revised National Curriculum in England and Wales (DfEE and QCA 1999) has blurred the valuable distinction between the notion of learning about technology (IT) and using technology to support learning (ICT) clearly described by the QCA & DfEE (1998 Teacher's Guide:19). The emphasis here is on using a computer to extend children's knowledge, understanding or skill in computer use itself. The technology is the focus of the learning.[iii]

Learning Tool is where your objective is to use computers in ways that support any aspect of children's learning other than *IT* itself. The focus here is not on the technology but on some other aspect of learning. This includes:

Curriculum Tool - Using computers in ways that help children develop skills, knowledge and understanding in a curriculum area other than *IT*. For example, you could use a word processing program to enhance children's language skills or graph generating program to enhance their ability to interpret data or provide a child who has 'special educational needs' with enhanced access to the curriculum.

Mathetic Tool - Using computers to develop children's ability to learn and enhance their approaches to learning; for example, using computers to encourage collaboration or help children reflect on their own learning. Explicitly teaching children how to teach other children to use particular software is a classic example of using computers as a *Mathetic Tool*.

Affective Tool - Using computers to support and enhance the affective aspects of children's learning such as their confidence, self-esteem or motivation.

Other is where your objective for using computers is not covered by *IT* or *Learning Tool*. Objectives for using computers that fall within this category may focus on practical aspects of the learning situation or the larger context in which computer use takes place. Using the computer as a reward or to impress a visitor to the classroom, such as an inspector, would fall into this category.

Clearly, in any one learning situation where computers are being used all three Foci will always apply to some extent because:

Teachers always have to consider management issues when planning and allocating activities (*Other*);

One cannot focus on learning to operate a computer (*IT*) in isolation from some content, which inevitably comes from some other curriculum area (*Learning Tool*);

When using a computer as a tool to support your learning (*Learning Tool*) you develop and/or reinforce your computing skills (*IT*);

Learning to become more effective learners (*Learning Tool*) should be an implicit part of teaching;

Any learning episode entails an element relating to the affective nature of the task (*Learning Tool*).

The important issue about the Focus is the relative balance between *IT*, *Learning Tool* and *Other*.

The Mode dimension – MrS S. (date .

The *Mode* dimension is concerned with the impact of computer use on the curriculum. The curriculum is taken here to cover all aspects of practice surrounding computer use including:

- content (which incorporates and goes beyond the explicit curriculum as set down in guidelines/curriculum documents but omits the *IT* curriculum – i.e. excluding aspects dealing with how to operate the computer/software);
- processes.

It is important to remember when applying the *Mode* that it applies only to those objectives specifically relating to *Learning Tool* within the *Focus* dimension (as illustrated in figure 4). Any use of ICT adds *IT* objectives to the curriculum content, but these are not relevant when thinking about the *Mode* of computer use within the CPF.

The *Mode* dimension of the CPF is sub-divided into three categories:

Support - Learning objectives (excluding those relating specifically to *IT*) remain the same but the process is automated in some way. *Support* is thus about improving efficiency and effectiveness without changing curriculum content. Using 'drill and skill' software or an 'integrated learning system' (ILS) fall into this category.

Extend - Curriculum content and/or process are different, but these changes *could* take place in a classroom context *without* a computer. For example, if you teach your children how to teach other children how to use some software and you have not previously taught them how to act as peer tutors in other contexts then this would fit into the *Extend* category. Whilst teaching children to be more effective peer tutors could operate in almost any subject area, it often originates in or is restricted to the context of computer use.

Transform - Curriculum content and/or process are different, and these changes *could not* have taken place in a classroom context *without* a computer. If children use multimedia authoring software to represent their ideas using images, video, text and hyperlinks then they are probably operating within the *Transform* category. You cannot create hypermedia without computers and the use of multiple media and hyperlinks transforms our notions of literacy (O'Neill 1998).

Linking the Computer Practice Framework and the planning cycle

At each stage of the planning cycle the CPF raises issues that can inform our practice. Many of the issues raised are similar, though with slightly different emphases, at each level of application of the planning cycle. This account therefore addresses all levels together, drawing out clear distinctions between the levels where necessary.

Planning

'the starting point in planning any activity is a clear understanding of the learning outcomes the teacher wants to achieve'

(McFarlane 1997:10)

The *Focus* dimension highlights the importance of being clear about the ICT focus within our planning. We need to distinguish between IT plans, in which our objectives relate specifically to learning about the technology, and plans in other curriculum areas where our objectives do not relate specifically to IT, but where ICT can enhance learning.

In long-term planning the only place where IT objectives should feature is in our IT scheme of work. This does not mean that ICT should not be used to support teaching in other areas; but when engaged in this stage of the planning cycle at this level we should set out the objectives to be met in each subject area rather than the means by which they will be met.

In short-term planning (e.g. a lesson plan) we should identify one key objective that each activity focuses on, with a small number of subsidiary objectives. At this level of planning we probably will mix IT objectives with those from other curriculum areas. However, it is crucial that subsidiary objectives for any activity enhance our key objective for that activity. We also need to consider how the activity will be implemented. A teacher in England might identify the following key objective in a lesson:

> To teach children that some materials are better thermal insulators than others.
> National Curriculum Key Stage 2 Science Sc3 1b (DfEE and QCA 1999:87)

This objective could be met in a number of different ways, including:

A. A chalk and talk lesson in which children are told about the thermal insulation properties of a number of materials and record this information in their books.

B. An investigation in which children set up a fair test where they record the rate of cooling of similar cups of water insulated by equal amounts of each material being tested. The children use traditional thermometers to record the water temperature in each cup every two minutes and plot graphs showing the temperature against time for each material.

C. An investigation in which the children set up a fair test where they measure the rate of cooling of similar cups of water insulated by equal amounts of each material being tested. The children use data logging equipment to measure the temperature of the water in each cup. The equipment records the temperature in each cup every second and plots this information on a time graph.

Each option has advantages and disadvantages. Option A is easy to prepare, would not require much equipment, and could be implemented more quickly than B or C. However, the children might not remember very long the information presented.

Options B and C both provide opportunities to address additional Science objectives from long-term planning, but will be more time consuming and require greater preparation and resources. Option C frees the children from carrying out the actual recording of temperature and plotting graphs, potentially providing them with more time to focus on interpreting results and thinking about which materials are the best insulators and why. The children's deeper level of engagement with thinking about the thermal insulation properties of the materials is likely to lead to a greater and more lasting understanding of those properties. Thus, Option C may be the best assuming that time and resources make it possible. This might lead the teacher to select the following subsidiary objectives, each clearly enhancing the key objective:

Subsidiary objectives:

a) To be able to make a fair test - National Curriculum Key Stage 2 Science Sc1 2d (DfEE and QCA 1999:83).

b) To be able to make systematic observations and measurements, including the use of ICT for data logging - National Curriculum Key Stage 2 Science Sc1 2f (DfEE and QCA 1999:83).

c) To be able to choose and use suitable measuring instruments for a task – National Curriculum Key Stage 2 Maths Ma3 4b (DfEE and QCA 1999:72).

d) To be able to interpret information and check that it is reasonable - National Curriculum Key Stage 2 ICT 1c (DfEE and QCA 1999:100).

Option C in this example hints at the potential for ICT to alter objectives. By freeing children from recording the temperature every two minutes and plotting graphs ICT provides them with the opportunity to take their analysis and investigation further.

The Mode dimension of the CPF highlights our need to consider the impact we want ICT to have on curriculum objectives within each subject. There are two important aspects: the impact of ICT on the sequence within which objectives are achievable and the degree to which ICT should change our objectives altogether.

The Mode dimension of the CPF indicates that ICT may support, extend or transform the objectives in each subject area. In English for example:

- a talking book could be used to support children's reading development;
- a word processor could be used to extend objectives relating to drafting and re-drafting;
- a hypermedia authoring package could be used to transform the mode of communication and our definition of literacy.

ICT may alter the order in which particular objectives can be tackled. For example, it is argued in the context of mathematics, that 'the age-relatedness of the present curriculum would disappear' (NCET 1993:6).

[ICT] gives young children access to large numbers, negative numbers and decimals, encourages a graphical approach to algebra, and provides a formal environment in which it is necessary to symbolise ideas. Thus computers and calculators challenge the very notion of a hierarchical curriculum;

(NCET 1993:27)

ICT can enable the introduction of new objectives (e.g. Scrimshaw 1997a) and alter the relative importance of existing ones (e.g. Cunningham 1997; NCET 1993). If we use ICT in ways that extend or transform learning objectives we should be aware that this may have a negative impact on external assessment outcomes. External assessments typically do not recognise or give credit for many of the objectives within ICT enabled curricula (Heppell 1999; Heppell 2000; Jones, et al. 1994).

In the planning stage of the cycle, particularly at short-term level, it is important to recognise we always have to balance our intentions with the reality of the situation in which we aim to implement our plans. For example, if we have no data logging equipment we cannot implement Option C in the example above, even if we thought it the best option. This need to work within the constraints of our particular context is reflected in the Focus dimension of the CPF, which recognises the importance of objectives only indirectly tied to specific curriculum outcomes. For example, when planning at the short-term level we must consider classroom management issues. There may be times when it is appropriate to use a computer-based activity as a way of occupying one 'learner' so that we can focus our attention on working with another learner. This is a legitimate objective, though seldom noted in planning documents, which is why it is important that it is validated within the CPF in the form of the *Other* category of the *Focus* dimension. *Other* objectives often relate to the realities of managing our learning context.

Implementing

The *Quantity* dimension of the CPF underlines the importance of ensuring that we have sufficient resources to enable the objectives identified in the planning stage to be met. The level of resourcing required depends on the extent to which our overall objectives relate to ICT, either because they are explicitly IT objectives or because they are objectives in other subject areas that ICT enables. If our focus is on using ICT to support learning (i.e. *Learning Tool* on the *Focus* dimension of the CPF) then the quantity of resources required will be higher than if our focus is to learn about the technology (i.e. *IT* on the *Focus* dimension). When our focus is on IT we 'only' have to learn how to use the technology, whereas when our focus is on using ICT as a tool to support learning we have to learn how to use the technology and also have to apply that 'knowledge'.

The quantity of resources we require also depends upon the way in which those resources are organised within our institution[iv]. The *Focus* dimension of the CPF indicates that whenever ICT is used in learning contexts all facets of that dimension apply to some degree. For example, whenever computers are used there will always be elements of learning how to use the technology (*IT*), using technology to support learning in other subject areas (*Learning Tool*) and using technology for pragmatic reasons indirectly linked to meeting learning objectives (*Other*). The issue is the relative importance that each of these should play. This gets to the heart of the debate, particularly in secondary schools, about whether IT skills should be taught in discrete IT lessons or as an integral part of the teaching of other subjects (e.g. Crawford 1997). There is no single 'right answer'. What is important is to be explicit at this stage of the planning cycle about the approach we shall take in our particular context and how this will be managed. At the long-term level this means establishing a clear policy about the nature, distribution and use of ICT resources across the whole institution. At the short-term level issues are slightly different, being constrained by the overall school policy on resource management and its impacts on 'classroom management'. However, the same basic issue arises about the degree to which IT skills should be taught in isolation or in the context in which they are needed.

The greater the emphasis on using technology as a *Learning Tool* the greater the potential there is for ICT to impact on the curriculum by *extending or transforming it*. Even where ICT is simply used to *support* learning it often requires organisational changes. For example, teachers have found that 'starting to use technology forced them to become more organized in what they do in classrooms' (Kerr 1991:131). The greater the curricular change, moving from *Support* through *Extend* to *Transform* on the *Mode* dimension, the greater need for changes in learning management.

Trilling and Hood (2001) argue that we need to *transform* education in order to capitalise on the potential of new technologies. They go on to identify that this represents 'a paradigm shift in educational practice.' (Trilling and Hood 2001:16). Change of this sort does not come easily and indeed there is substantial evidence that 'computers are more likely to be used when they fit easily into existing methods of teaching and classroom organisation.' (Chalkey and Nicholas 1997:104) – i.e. when they are being used to *support* the existing curriculum.

An important factor in the management and use of resources is the level of staff confidence and competence in using the technology. This includes their IT competence, but more importantly their understanding of the ways in which ICT can be used to support learning and of the different management strategies that this may require (Scrimshaw 1997b; Twining and McCormick 1999). The greater the level of staff confidence and competence in using the technology the more likely it is that we can use technology in ways that *Extend* and *Transform* the curriculum.

Assessing

Assessment fulfils a number of roles (Goldstein 1994; Pollard and Tann 1993), but should be primarily concerned with improving our learners' performance (Twining and Richards 1999). One way in which it can do this is by helping to maintain the teachers' and learners' attention on the key objectives they are trying to meet (as identified in the plan phase of the cycle). Thus, assessment criteria need to be closely linked to learning objectives. Where the focus of an activity is on achieving IT objectives that should also be the focus of the assessment criteria. Where ICT is being used as a *Learning Tool* our assessment criteria should link to the subject objectives that ICT is intended to help the learners achieve. One difficulty is that the use of ICT can distort a learner's achievements in some areas. Trend, et al. (1999:23) describe how the use of spell and grammar checkers can impact on assessment of children's literacy development: 'They might, for example, produce prose with immaculate spelling and sophisticated grammar without increasing their understanding of literacy'. The key here is in being able to distinguish between the learner's competence in IT (e.g. being able to use the spell and grammar checker) and in the curriculum area that ICT is supporting (e.g. knowledge of spelling and grammar).

Where ICT is *extending* or *transforming* the curriculum it is clear that the assessment criteria we use should also be extended or transformed to reflect the changed nature of the learning objectives (McFarlane 1997; Wiske, et al. 1988). Otherwise, as Hoffman (1996 p52) has pointed out, even the 'most successful technology integration may look like a dismal failure if assessed using traditional methods'. This is illustrated by Heppell's racing car analogy:

> Imagine a nation of horse riders with a clearly defined set of riding capabilities. In one short decade the motor car is invented and within that same decade many children become highly competent drivers extending the boundaries of their travel as well as developing entirely new leisure pursuits (like stock-car racing and hot-rodding). At the end of the decade government ministers want to assess the true impact of automobiles on the nation's capability. They do it by putting everyone back on the horses and checking their dressage, jumping and trotting as before. Of course, we can all see that it is ridiculous,
>
> (Heppell 1994:154)

ICT can change the relative importance of aspects of 'traditional' curriculum objectives and can introduce new ones.

Even where ICT appears to be used to *support* the curriculum, it may alter aspects of the task, thus necessitating changes to assessment criteria. In our Science example, the use of data logging equipment supports the original objective (learning about the thermal insulation properties of materials) but also alters the task that the children are carrying out by relieving them of the need to perform the measurements or draw the graphs. This is reflected in the subsidiary objectives and thus should also be reflected in the assessment criteria. In this particular case it is clear that the process the children have engaged with will have been changed as a result of the use of data logging equipment. This, like the example of the spell and grammar checker, highlights the importance of your assessment looking at the learning process as well as what the learners produce.

The *Mode* dimension deliberately separates out the process and product elements of the curriculum in order to highlight that ICT does not just alter the products that derive from children's learning activities but often impacts on the processes through which learning takes place. For example, a group of children who are working on a multimedia presentation, such as a set of web pages or a PowerPoint slideshow, may work in a truly collaborative manner, which results in one communal group output. In trying to assess the children's learning on this activity it would not be sufficient to focus exclusively on that group product. You would need to take into account the ways in which the children worked to develop it and how their individual contributions reflected their individual knowledge, skills and understanding. The final product tells you nothing about each individual child's learning; for that you need to look at the process and each child's part in it. Assessment of the process through which the children produced their web pages or PowerPoint slideshow tells you much more about their learning than the product itself.

Evaluating

Evaluation is important because it allows us to refine our teaching by comparing our intended outcomes (planning) with those that were achieved (assessment), as illustrated in figure 1. This distinction between what we intend and what is achieved applies equally to the dimensions of the CPF: it is important to distinguish between what we intended in relation to each dimension of the CPF and what was achieved on those dimensions. For example, we might plan to use a data handling program to help children gain a better understanding of the most appropriate ways to analyse some data but end up with the children spending most of their time learning how to operate the software or typing in the data without having time for analysis and reflection.

The three dimensions of the CPF provide a framework (see figure 5) that can support us during the evaluation stage of the planning cycle.

			Intended	Achieved
Quantity	Proportion of the available time when **computers were in use**		%	%
Focus	Proportion of time during which **computers were in use and the** *Focus* **was**	IT	%	%
		Learning Tool	%	%
		Other	%	%
Mode	Proportion of the time during which **computers were being used as a** *Learning Tool* **and the** *Mode* **was**	*Support*	%	%
		Extend	%	%
		Transform	%	%

Figure 5: A framework for evaluating the extent to which our intended computer use matches our actual computer use – based on the Computer Practice Framework

This framework can be applied at each level of the planning cycle to inform future planning and hence enhance our future implementations and achievements.

Conclusion

Making effective use of computers in education is a complex process, which requires a clear vision about why we are using computers and the impact we want them to have on the curriculum. A lack of clarity, or worse still a conflict of views about why we are using computers in education has reduced the impact of the substantial levels of investment that have been made in educational computing over the last 20+ years. However, a clear vision on its own is not enough. It needs to be moulded by the constraints of our particular context and fed into our planning cycle so that we can develop realistic plans that set out both what we aim to achieve and how we aim to achieve it. The Computer Practice Framework (CPF) can be used as a tool to help us as we work through the stages of the planning cycle. By so doing it can help us to make more effective use of our ICT resources and thus help us achieve our vision for computer use in education.

References

Anderson, R., T. Hansen, et al. (1979) 'Instructional computing: acceptance and rejection by secondary school teachers.' *Sociology of Work and Occupations* 6: 227-250

Blease, D. and L. Cohen (1990) *Coping with Computers: an ethnographic study in primary classrooms*. London, Paul Chapman

Chalkey, T. W. and D. Nicholas (1997) 'Teachers' use of information technology: observations of primary school practice.' *Aslib Proceedings* 49(4): 97-107.

Cloke, C. (2000) 'Planning to use ICT, factors which influence teachers.' *ESRC ICT & Pedagogy*

Crawford, R. (1997) *Managing Information Technology in Secondary Schools*, London: Routledge

Cunningham, P. (1997) 'IT and thinking skills in humanities', in A. McFarlane (Ed) *Information Technology and Authentic Learning: Releasing the potential of computers in the primary classroom*, London: Routledge

Dearing, R. (1997) *Higher Education in the Learning Society: Report of the National Committee of Enquiry into Higher Education*

DfEE (2000) *Information and Communications Technology in Schools*, England: 2000, DfEE

DfEE and QCA (1999) *The National Curriculum: Handbook for primary teachers in England Key stages 1 and 2*. London, DfEE & QCA

Galton, M., L. Hargreaves, et al. (1999) *Inside the Primary Classroom: 20 years on*. London, Routledge

Goldstein, H. (1994) 'Educational Quality and Student Achievement', in P. Ribbins and E. Burridge (Eds) *Improving Education: Promoting quality in schools*, London: Cassell

Heppell, S. (1994) 'Multimedia and learning: Normal children, normal lives and real change', in J. Underwood (Ed) Computer based learning: Potential into practice, London: David Fulton Publishers

Heppell, S. (1999) 'Computers Creativity Curriculum and Children...' *Times Educational Supplement*, London

Heppell, S. (2000) 'eLearning: How might eLearning really change educational policy and practice?', *RSA / Design Council 'Education Futures' journal*

Hoffman, B. (1996) 'What Drives Successful Technology Planning?', *JITTE* 5(1/2): 43-55

Jameson, J. (2000) 'Editorial.' *ALT-J* 8(3): 2-3

Jones, B. F., Valdez, G., Nowakowski, J. and Rasmussen, C. (1994) *Designing Learning and Technology for Educational Reform*, Oak Brook, IL: North Central Regional Educational Laboratory

Kerr, S., T. (1991) 'Lever and Fulcrum: Educational technology in teachers' thought and practice', *Teachers College Record* 93(1): 114-136

Kerrey, B., J. Isakson, et al. (2000) *The Power of the Internet for Learning: Moving from*

Promise to Practice. Report of the Web-Based Education Commission to the President and the Congress of the United States. Washington DC, Web-Based Education Commission to the President and the Congress of the United States

McFarlane, A. (1997) 'Where are we and how did we get here?' in McFarlane (Ed) *Information Technology and Authentic Learning: Releasing the potential of computers in the primary classroom.* London, Routledge: 1-12

Moseley, D., S. Higgins, et al. (1999) *Ways forward with ICT: Effective pedagogy using Information and Communications Technology for Literacy and Numeracy in Primary Schools.* Newcastle, University of Newcastle

NCET (1993) *The Future Curriculum with IT*, Coventry: NCET

OFSTED (1997) *Information Technology in English Schools: A commentary on Inspection Findings 1995-96*

OFSTED (1999) *Annual report of Her Majesties Chief Inspector of Schools 1998/99*, London, HMSO

O'Neill, B. (1998) 'New Ways of Telling: Multimedia Authoring in the Classroom' in Monteith (Ed) *IT for Learning Enhancement*, Exeter, Intellect: 141-152

Pollard, A. and Tann, S. (1993) *Reflective Teaching in the Primary School: A handbook for the classroom*, 2nd Edition, London: Cassell

Preston, C., M. Cox, et al. (2000) *Teachers As Innovators: An evaluation of the motivation of teachers to use information and communications technologies.* London, MirandaNet

QCA and DfEE (1998) *Information Technology: A scheme of work for Key Stages 1 and 2.* London, Qualification and Curriculum Authority (QCA)

Scrimshaw, P. (1997a) 'Computers and the teacher's role', in B. Somekh and N. Davis (Eds) *Using Information Technology effectively in Teaching and Learning: Studies in Pre-Service and In-Service Teacher Education*, London: Routledge

Scrimshaw, P. (1997b) *Preparing for the Information Age: Synoptic Report of the Education Departments Superhighways Initiative*, Milton Keynes: The Open University

Stevenson, D., I. Anderson, et al. (1997) *Information and Communications Technology in UK Schools - An independent Enquiry*, London, Independent ICT in School Commission

Taylor, C. (1997) in B. Somekh and N. Davis (Eds) *Using Information Technology effectively in Teaching and Learning: Studies in Pre-Service and In-Service Teacher Education*, London: Routledge

Trend, R., N. Davis, et al. (1999) *Information and Communications Technology*, London, Letts Educational

Trilling, B. and P. Hood (2001) 'Learning, Technology, and Educational Reform in the Knowledge Age or 'We're Wired, Webbed, and Windowed, Now What?' in C. Paechter, R. Edwards, R. Harrison and P. Twining (Eds) *Learning, Space and Identity*, London, Paul Chapman Publishing Ltd: 7-30

Twining, P. (1995) 'Making Barriers Explicit: Some Problems with the Computer Innovation Literature', *Technology and Teacher Education Annual, 1995: Proceedings of SITE 95 - Sixth International Conference of the Society for Information Technology and Teacher Education (SITE)*, San Antonio, Texas, Association for the Advancement of Computing in Education

Twining, P. (2001b) 'Pedagogic re-engineering: issues surrounding the use of new media to support a move from 'didactic' to 'constructivist' models of transaction on an Open University course', in M. Selinger and J. Wynn (Eds) *Educational Technology and the impact on teaching and learning*, Oxford, Research Machines: 54-60

Twining, P. (2001a) 'Planning to use ICT in schools?' *Education 3-13* 29(1)

Twining, P. and R. McCormick (1999) *Learning Schools Programme: Developing Teachers' Information Communication Technology Competence In The Support Of Learning*. 10th International Conference of The Society for Information Technology & Teacher Education, San Antonio, Texas, AACE

Twining, P. and C. Richards (1999) *Learning Schools Programme: Teaching in Primary.* Milton Keynes, The Open University

Underwood, J. (1988) 'An investigation of teacher intents and classroom outcomes in the use of information-handling packages.' *Computer Education* 12(1): 91-100

Underwood, J. and M. Monteith, Eds. (1998) *Supporting the Wider Teaching Community: Case studies in IT INSET*. Coventry, ITTE & BECTA

Wiske, M. S., Zodhiates, P., Wilson, B., Gordon, M., Harvey, W., Krensky, L., Lord, B., Watt, M. and Williams, K. (1988) *How Technology Affects Teaching*, Cambridge, Massachusetts: Educational Technology Centre, Harvard Graduate School of Education

---

[i]Further Education in England

[ii]The school day is taken to mean time when children are in school but excludes play times, lunch times, after school clubs etc.. The number of children using a computer is irrelevant (for this dimension). The number of computers in use is irrelevant (for this dimension). If a computer is being used with children (even if they are not controlling the keys/mouse) that counts as it being used by the children.

[iii]Throughout the remainder of this chapter I will use IT and ICT to refer to learning about the technology and using the technology to support learning respectively.

[iv]For discussion of alternative models of ICT resourcing in schools see: (Taylor 1997; Twining and Richards 1999; Twining 2001a).

Curriculum Enrichment: using online resources, balancing creativity with the readily available

Libby Jared

Introduction

Over the last few years there has been much excited talk about the Internet and the possibilities it opens up for teaching and learning. Indeed, seldom a day passes when the newspapers do not include something on the subject. In quieter moments away from all the hype, a pause for reflection provides opportunities for considering the possible impact new technologies might have to enrich the present-day curriculum, thus influencing both school and higher education courses. Through discussing Internet-related issues, I intend to illustrate the potential of, and to investigate the concepts behind, using online resources.

It could not be claimed that the issues surrounding using on-line resources are nearly as many as the number of online resources themselves; supposedly the number of web pages published doubles every four months (Ager 2000). However, it is important that we discover how teachers, student teachers and pupils can make best use of the unending number of resources 'out there'. There is a need to debate what specific teaching is needed on how to make best use and how this can be learned. We should also investigate the significance of using such resources that enrich and extend an inclusive curriculum for all pupils with Special Educational Needs, including the most able. The list continues to grow: a more recent phenomenon is the contribution from home use. There is a need to know about the impact which home computer use is making to pupils' learning at a time when an increasing number of homes are connecting to the Internet, (often with higher specification resources than most schools can keep abreast with and with a greater individual access). Indeed, it may be that the Internet can enrich not only the school curriculum but the life experiences of both pupils and teachers.

In seeking to address such issues, this chapter will make specific reference to a mathematics web site appropriate to learners and teachers (aged 5 to 95!) - the NRICH web site (http://www.nrich.maths.org.uk). This is the web site that I initially helped to establish and launch in September 1996. It is worthwhile pausing here to give a brief account of how the site came to be set up and its subsequent growth.

In late 1995 four people sat round a table mulling over an idea. We were discussing ways in which new technologies might be harnessed to provide free, stimulating mathematics resources available to every school in the land by invoking just a few mouse clicks. We recognised that in a full and busy classroom, with the best will in the world it was often difficult for teachers to give sufficient time to stretching the most able in mathematics. Here then was the opportunity to help both teachers and pupils alike. We wanted to provide new material, electronically, via a monthly magazine and a communication system where pupils interested in exploring and discussing maths with fellow enthusiasts could do this in a supportive atmosphere and not be given (as some are) the 'nerd' tag. All that was then needed was money to pay people for writing and managing the site.

This was moving into new territories but a proposal was written and eventually having approached several public and private enterprises, monies and sponsorship were finally secured. NRICH had been born. (It actually literally took around nine months from the initial idea to seeing it come on-line!). NRICH took its first steps aimed at Key Stage 3 classes and had a pilot year with 34 Norfolk schools managed by the county's mathematics advisory staff. (At this stage, NRICH was (conveniently) an acronym of **N**orfolk, The **R**oyal **I**nstitution, **C**ambridge University and **H**omerton College, the four originators' workplaces, which coincidentally and fortuitously conveys the enrichment aim). A year later its 'headquarters' moved to its present home now the Faculty of Education at the University of Cambridge and NRICH went (inter)national - the N could move from Norfolk to **N**ational - and began to have resources across all key stages. The site now included the infamously named Bernard's Bag for primary pupils. The bag held investigations that Bernard had previously tried with 'real' pupils and which could be undertaken by all the class with the opportunity for the more able to extend the work further. By providing a commentary and teacher's notes this started to become a popular part of the site, but nevertheless it took another year to find further funding and personnel before launching the Primary site (NRICH Prime) in October 1998.

Ever since, the entire NRICH website has grown considerably under an expanding and innovative team. This team includes a director who manages all the personnel involved and has overall editorial control, a primary co-ordinator, a person who liaises and trains the undergraduates responding to pupil questions and a group of computer experts who design the pages and undertake the site's technical aspects. With new resources going on the web site on the 1st of every month and pupils being invited to send solutions by 21st of month for publication just nine days later, there are numerous deadlines constantly to be met. The schedule is well rehearsed and the site established.

The reader is asked to bear in mind that though this is a web site specific to just one core subject area, mathematics, there is no reason why the ideas associated with this cannot be transferred to other subject areas.

Background
Although some schools had begun to obtain Internet links in the early 1990s, these were the exception rather than the rule. In the latter part of 1997 the government

announced its intention to have all schools connected to the Internet by the year 2002 '…perhaps 75% of teachers and 50% of pupils…' will be using their own email addresses (BECTa 1998). The Department for Education and Skills (DfES) in its annual statistical survey of ICT provision in schools, published October 2002, cites that over 99% of both Secondary and Primary schools are connected to the Internet, (DfES 2002). However, analysis is still required to establish the nature of these Internet links and how many classrooms are actually connected. Incidentally, the same survey provides data indicating that 57% Primary, 75% Secondary and 67% Special School teachers have an e-mail account provided and funded by an educational organisation. For pupils, figures of 12%, 43% and 15% respectively are given for individual (educational) e-mail addresses. Although below the original target, I believe that there has been a shift away from providing pupils with their own e-mail address as a precautionary measure against outside misuse.

The consultation document, *Connecting the Learning Society* (DfEE 1997), revealed plans to instigate with public/private partnership a National Grid for Learning (NGfL). The executive summary described the grid's two-prong purpose: 'A way of finding and using on-line learning and teaching materials' and 'A mosaic of inter-connecting networks and education services based on the Internet which will support teaching, learning, training and administration in schools, colleges, universities, libraries, the workplace and homes'.

In April 2001, the consultation document, *Curriculum OnLine*, was published with the belief that 'The use of digital technology for improving delivery of education has enormous potential to raise standards …'. In his introduction, the Secretary of State for Education explained the vision. 'We want these (*online resources*) to be capable of being used with Interactive Whiteboards, PCs and over digital television, so that they can contribute to teachers' lesson planning as flexibly as possible, as well as supporting homework and family learning. And we want these materials to form a coherent whole.' (DfES 2001)

From the outset, there was, and still remains, an expectation that electronic sources will transform the curriculum of the future – be it a curriculum for pupils, teachers, parents or life-long learners. A look into the future brings with it an opening up of the boundaries where such a curriculum might be met. Certainly there is no possibility that it is going to be confined to the classroom. Indeed we can meet a 'curriculum without walls' (Bentley 1998).

Having passed through the prototype and other developmental stages, a relaunch of the Virtual Teacher Centre (the online area of the NGfL) was made in January 2001. Since first announcements in 1997 we have seen a rapid growth both to the number of internet users and the facilities which web sites can afford. Not surprisingly one of the VTC's features is the Teacher Resource Exchange, designed to help teachers share and develop teaching resources and activities. However there is still a difference in online features being available and being used – getting all members of a conferencing group to fully participate is difficult as many moderators would testify. This challenge will surely remain for many years to come.

Training perspective

Potter and Mellar, whilst working with a group of practising teachers to devise effective in-service training to use the Internet for Curriculum work, analysed findings from a study begun in 1997. Out of the 35 teachers involved although 26 felt confident working with the Web and 23 enjoyed working with the Internet in School, 24 chose low or very low for integration of the Internet in the Curriculum. (Potter & Mellar 2000). This I believe is the starting point for many teacher trainees.

If asked to complete an ICT skills survey at the beginning of their course, it would be surprising if now, virtually all post graduate and undergraduate trainees did not gleefully tick off any box which includes the word 'Internet'. Many arrive with an 'unknowing familiarity' with the Internet, keen on using Search Engines and all that it entails. Most trainees will have had substantial experiences both in the requirement to use it for academic study – observing teaching (whilst being taught) and participating in learning, with online resources – and personal use much of which might have included surfing and chat room activities. However such experiences alone are probably insufficient to make effective use within an educational context. It is only as one begins to analyse the contribution that the Internet is making to their teaching and their pupils' learning, that the idea of 'the more you learn the less you know' appears.

It is interesting to consider the trainees' views of the Internet judging by the following list, compiled by a group of teacher trainees, as to why teachers might want to search the Internet to:
- locate helpful articles in a whole host of educational topics
- keep informed about government news and policies
- keep abreast of the latest National Curriculum developments
- view, download or order official documentation
- brush up on subject knowledge or conduct research
- look for helpful advice on school purchasing decisions
- join in a discussion forum to share best practice
- keep in touch with unions
- find assessment aids, such as guides to attainment levels
- consult Schemes of Work
- look at examples of Units of Work
- download lesson plans
- print out worksheets
- find online activities for use in the classroom, such as interactive Literacy exercises .... or Numeracy games and Puzzles

The ordering of this list is interesting. It begins with a strong emphasis on professional development. It moves on towards obtaining lesson plans and worksheets – in essence the Internet is a shop where one might go in and get things off the shelf. Only at the very end is there explicit mention of the classroom and a leaning towards learning. Although this order might have been totally unintentional, this could present cause for concern. On first sight, there is a worry that this list, dominated by ready-made materials, may become too seductive, pushing the trainees' innovation and specific class appropriateness into second place. Balancing creativity with the readily available is a life skill we all need to develop. A focus on critically reviewing online resources will be essential in achieving this.

An online classroom resource - one web site, a multitude of uses

It seems appropriate to consider some of the concepts which lie behind using online resources as a learning tool and to draw out the impact that these might have on teaching and learning. In order to do this, you are asked to consider the variety of uses that teachers and young people can make of the NRICH web site. Note that as with any other web site, a consequence of the Internet's dynamic nature means that there will likely be further changes to the site, beyond the present description offered here.

Within the descriptions, reference will sometimes be made to evaluation reports. These were reflective studies, undertaken to gauge the project's work and the impact it was having both in school and at home. I conducted two internal evaluations (Jared 1997, 1998); the first (small scale) at the end of the pilot year, the second one year later when the project had gone worldwide. The evaluations included questionnaires and targeted interviews from NRICH users and other interested parties. For the second year as an innovation, the questionnaire was set up on the web site and replies received virtually. At the end of the third year an external evaluation was undertaken (Jones & Simons 1999).

NRICH describes itself as a mathematics 'net-workshop' which offers pupils of all ages who enjoy the challenges of mathematics, the opportunity to participate either with friends in a school mathematics club or individually (via school or home). It is a virtual meeting place for young minds to share ideas and collaborate. Web-board conferencing between school pupils and university students enables the pupils to have their mathematical questions answered and to discuss their own ideas with university students through 'Ask NRICH', the 'Ask a Mathematician' Answering service. Pupils can also discuss mathematics in the 'NRICHtalk' mailing list whilst teachers have their own in 'NRICHsupport', a self support 'chat' group where views and experiences can be exchanged.

Currently there are two interrelating divisions to NRICH: NRICH Prime (broadly for primary aged children) and NRICH Club (broadly meeting the 11-18 curriculum). Both have a monthly magazine style with mathematics problems to try, articles to read, games to play (not the 'normal' zapping the alien type of computer game but ones which involve logical thinking, which are described on screen but then played person against person) news etc. The mathematics problems come in all shapes and sizes: many are investigational with Bernard's Bag problems perhaps the more open-ended, whilst Penta Problems, Monthly Six, and More Challenging Problems are more recognisable as 'ordinary' mathematics problems.

The magazine is published on the 1st of each month and pupils are invited to send in solutions by the 21st. The best of these solutions, either from individuals or groups, are then published (and acknowledged) within the solutions section the following month. The interpretation of 'best' is judged according to how well the pupils have thought out, explained and justified their methods. A published solution may lead to someone finding a more elegant one, in which case this may also be published later and thus the 'conversation' continues.

Consider for one moment the issue of age. In mathematics generally, there is a wide age range in pupils' abilities to understand the concepts within the hierarchical nature of the subject. Whilst the original intention was to plug an apparent hole and provide a rich resource for the most able pupils, opportunities exist for other pupils (and adults!) to tackle the challenges initially aimed for an earlier age group, as they become older. Each of the problems is annotated with a symbol relating to the curriculum's Key Stage – i.e. the problem can successfully be answered with the mathematical knowledge from the indicated key stage. However there are problems which can be approached with ever increasing sophistication and these have a blue symbol for the 'sky's the limit'. There is no bar on the pupil's age for a solution to be accepted. Neither should it be thought that by 'pigeon-holing' problems anyone should not undertake and enjoy a problem outside the specified age group. Some very young children are extremely good at maths, some adults become interested many years after they have left school. The intention of the web site is not only to enrich the normal maths experience in school but also to support everyone's ability to enrich themselves. We simply must not be deterred if at the age of 50 we find ourselves working at a problem first intended for an eight-year-old! There are many such problems on the web site.

Each 'issue' of the magazine is archived in the Resource Bank, where all past material is classified according to topic, with a search tree and a keyword searching facility. Once the solutions have been published, the problems are stored individually, with links to their solution and similar problems. Having a little peep at the solutions sometimes helps us to understand the mathematics behind the problem and provide the individual enrichment for life-long learning. All the published materials are currently freely available on the Internet.

It is important to realise that whilst all the above refers to the Internet and a web site, much of the time is spent 'off line'.. Material can be downloaded and problems worked on in the 'ordinary' classroom. Just from this web site's description, and again to stress that it serves only as one internet example, a list of opportunities (bringing alongside new concepts), which would not otherwise be available in the non-Internet classroom, immediately spring to mind. Each opportunity will in turn have an effect on teaching and learning. Such a list could include:

- receiving a regular source of new material – simultaneously with every other school pupil in the world (with access to an Internet link);
- access to an archive of previous material – a need to become proficient in searching and retrieval skills;
- collaboration between pupils in or out of the same classroom, school, country;
- pupils (in this case) comparing strategies by studying solutions sent in by other schools and the ability to improve on a solution leading to an insight into the nature of proof;
- networking – putting self-minded people in touch with others, be they pupils or teachers, schools or individuals;

- providing an expert to answer those 'niggling' questions;
- catering for pupils of a specific ability;

A source of new material

In itself there maybe nothing innovative about finding material published on the web site, similar problems could easily be found in a textbook. Thus one might claim that this part of the web site is just a 'glorified' textbook, especially when the pages are printed out. However it is the instantaneous global aspect which is important and creates the difference. To many pupils there is still a sense of excitement that other school children across the other side of the world might be doing the same problem during the same school day. As one primary teacher said: '*Although my class do investigations and problem solving often, they are very impressed by the global nature of these problems and the fact that anyone in the world can have a go at them.*' (Jared 1998).

The problems can reach every single pupil for whom they are intended, new ones appearing monthly.. An analogy would be to expect everyone to go into the bookshop monthly to purchase a book (and which would need to be paid for). There are other advantages to this global nature for as one teacher replied: '*(I am) very grateful for the service. I feel less isolated now that I have discovered the site and have been encouraged to let the children innovate and experiment more.*' (Jared 1998).

Access to an archive of material

Because the material is available electronically, it can be easily stored in a variety of ways. This might be simply to store previous months one after the other just as a pile of monthly magazines might be kept but more useful though is to 'tear' the pages out and store by, say, key stage and mathematics topic. Either means will require searching and retrieval skills, skills which have really grown in prominence since databases, CD-ROMS and the Internet have come on stream. This is a good example of the purpose providing the need that all pupils should be taught these skills from as early an age as necessary.

Collaboration

Collaboration is no longer a new concept. It does not need any computer technology to get pupils working together on a task; such work can easily be undertaken in any classroom and pupils can recount their findings to their peers. What is new is that for the user internet facilities can act as a catalyst to initiate or develop teaching and learning styles. Within one year of meeting the NRICH web site, teachers were reporting a change in the way of working: '*(The) department is now more willing to try puzzles out as part of their teaching*' and '*More peer interaction*'. (Jared 1998).

Perhaps at this juncture, it is worth making a further comment on collaboration where existing boundaries might be removed: a specific problem can be challenging or appealing to a range of ages. Material taken from the Internet providing a ready-made set of problems can be the means for a teacher to set up school maths clubs and other extra curricular activities. Hence instead of global virtual meetings, there is the potential locally for a variety of pupils interested and intent on working on some mathematics to actually meet up in person. These human groupings can either be from the same school or a cluster of schools, for whom the usual school structure might otherwise be prohibitive.

Comparing strategies, examining solutions

The ICT national curriculum for schools has placed great measure on selecting different tools and materials to present a specific piece of work. In effect, there may well be no single correct way of communicating the information; discussing the various forms of presentation is a vital part of the work. On one occasion two sixth form students certainly did this when they sent in eight different (and correct) solutions to a NRICH problem. By seeing a variety of solutions pupils are realising that there may be different ways to solve one problem. Although one method may be more efficient than another, the different methods may be equally valid.

It is doubtful that a few years ago teachers would have considered that another school could provide the means to discuss with their own class the quality of class solutions. But now with sets of solutions published, one school can look at solutions from another to compare, to judge and debate whether their own might be improved. Reflecting on the quality of a solution is a learning skill to be harnessed and the Internet provides the means for this. One teacher described how the pupils would compare the published solutions with their own work. There were also occasions when pupils would revisit the solutions and further extend their own work. In the 1998 evaluation report, one girl aged twelve commented: *'I look at how different users have used different methods to reach the solution (and see if I have been mentioned). If I got one wrong or I found one problem difficult, so I didn't send off my solution, I'd look at the answer, so I can learn something from it.'* (Jared 1998)

The general accessibility of a variety of solutions provides a springboard for the consideration of mathematical proof. A Times Educational Article of 13.3.98 entitled "Prove it" reported on the results of a survey carried out by Celia Hoyles and Lulu Healy. The opening paragraph read 'After six years of national curriculum maths, high-achieving students are overwhelmingly unable to engage with proof'. Hoyles herself believes that 'If pupils have not learned proof by the time they get to year 10, I am really sure it is too late' (Hoyles and Healy 1998). For some pupils (and adults) this might not need to be a necessary skill, but for those students who wish to study mathematics further, many find it difficult to provide mathematical proofs when required. It is still early days yet to announce that a website can provide the means to improve pupils' ability for proof, though encouragement comes from one teacher who reported that within one year his pupils had a better idea of the rigour required for mathematical proofs.

Networking people

The Internet can provide an easy means of networking people both technically through mailing lists built into the services provided by a site, or simply mailing lists per se, or physically setting up clubs. Many teachers feel much less isolated now; asking the whole world which book(s) they would recommend for a particular area of study can quickly bring more than a few replies. Like-minded people are brought together. Pupils between themselves can communicate about their mathematical ideas. Being involved brings home to pupils simultaneously the huge global nature of the Internet and the smallness of the world.

Ask an expert

Online communications can allow for a pupil to 'post' a question and find it answered by an expert. A private (though monitored) dialogue can continue between the two until the 'conversation' ceases, at which time it may be posted on the site for everyone to read. Whilst some teachers are slightly worried that this might help pupils to cheat in their homework and coursework, in reality the slight delay in answering a problem generally pushes it out of time for homework.

The potential for using the Internet in this way was quickly realised. The National Council for Educational Technology (NCET, now BECTa) stated in 1995: 'It is likely that e-mail access to mathematicians in universities - 'Ask an Expert' scheme - would prove to be extremely popular with schools (and not just for mathematics). There is also scope here for accessing expert help with homework and for linking gifted students over the Internet to work collaboratively'. (NCET 1995).

Catering for the most able pupils

The previous quote connects well to the final item on the list. Freeman describes enrichment to be 'the deliberate rounding out of the basic curriculum subjects with ideas and knowledge that enable a pupil to be aware of the wider context of a subject area.' (Freeman 1998). That many of our most able pupils, for many understandable reasons, have not been academically stretched in (some) lessons is one view which has held from the dim and distant past to the present day. Given the present UK government's drive to raise standards in schools, there must be some credence given to this view. In this new information age there may be great potential for educational innovations to make opportunities available to all children irrespective of where they live or go to school. Undoubtedly the Internet has enabled provision for gifted and talented children of a type, and on a scale, never before possible. Given the comparatively recent rise in use of the Internet, the effect of using online resources on the talented and gifted is not well researched. Whether the Internet will provide the solution so long sought by teachers of able children, is as yet neither known nor well researched. (Beardon et al. 1999).

In all the descriptions above, the most able child has been at the forefront of services provided. Using the Internet as a means of posting material provides plenty of opportunities to publish material aimed at a specific ability. Busy classrooms and large class sizes can mean that on occasions the most able are left unchallenged. Having ever-changing 'difficult' problems can provide an external stimulus that in turn can become internal.

The Learning Place

This chapter has attempted to address the issues posed at the beginning. One still predominantly remains – the part played by home use. A considered discussion would merit a chapter in itself, but one cannot leave this alone without some mention of the implications that surround home ownership.

Given that there is surely an inevitability to the Internet becoming a 'natural' part of modern life, the central claim that good educational web sites will add to the present school curriculum must have some foundation. However it is more than this. The school curriculum does not start and stop with the classroom door. In the widest sense this has always been true but now we are in an age where many pupils have Internet access at home and will not only find sites such as NRICH for themselves but interact with it, learning something new on the way. We hear in the media how the new technologies are changing the whole notion of the 'adult workplace' but with an increasing number of homes becoming 'connected' the 'pupil learningplace' is also significantly changing.

Before one is carried away by the rhetoric, work recently undertaken by Furlong et al. on how young people utilise ICT at home and school raises some fundamental points. These preliminary findings have highlighted a range of social factors which are affecting home use – and as the research suggests, unequal opportunities may well impinge on the UK government's vision that the NGfL will bring an egalitarian future. However there is evidence that some advantaged children (in terms of for example financial, cultural, boys rather than girls) 'are well placed to exploit the benefits of the promised revolution, and their learning experiences at home will fit them well for the technologically rich but unpredictable world of the future'. (Furlong et al. 2000).

Inevitably, home users of NRICH must fit into the advantaged bracket in order to utilise the web site. That acknowledged, there is evidence, from the internal NRICH evaluations, to suggest a breaking down of boundaries. There is scope for undertaking interesting research on the home only user. 'The Internet has opened up the possibility for children to find, in their own home, "school work" not set by their teacher, but which captures their interest to pursue. The phenomenon of a child taking responsibility for determining their own learning might not be too far away'. (Jared 1998). The research carried out for the 1998 evaluation partly involved posting an electronic questionnaire on the site and inviting interested parties to fill it in. Although recognising that the pupil replies were sent electronically, allowing a strong assumption that the sample is naturally biased towards the home user, even so a breakdown of these pupil responses still has a story to tell (see table 1). From the 68 pupil replies, around two-fifths of the sample saw the problems first on a home computer. Of these 27 pupils it would appear that 13 (which in this small sample is around 50%) not only saw the mathematics problems at home first but were doing the problems only at home, though not necessarily alone but working at times with friends and family. For these pupils in 1998 there appeared to be little school involvement, and one could suggest that they are devising their own timetable for learning. To what effect poor internet access generally to school had on this one cannot tell.

First see problems	Of 27 pupils who first see at home, problems undertaken at:		Of 41 pupils who first see at school, problems undertaken at:	
Home 27 School 41	Lessons only	1	Lessons only	5
	Lessons & Home	8	Lessons & Home	14
	Home only	13	Home only	4
	Maths club	0	Maths club	6
	Maths club & home	3	Maths club & home	4
	Maths club & lesson	2	Maths club lesson	6
			No response	2

Table 1: *Response to where problems were first seen and subsequently where problems were undertaken.*

Consider for one moment the effect of the following words written by a student, aged twelve, for the 1998 NRICH evaluation: *'I enjoy using 'NRICH'. I have sent off my solutions three times and been mentioned for having the correct solution. I have been passing on the word about "NRICH" and given the access address. One person I told, is a maths teacher at another secondary school who has tried one with his pupils. They all say it's great!!!'* Who precisely is the learner in this context? Who is the teacher? Have we gone topsy-turvy?

Conclusion

I am of course not impartial. I believe that the Internet will undoubtedly enrich the lives of those who embrace it in a workable and effective way. It does have the potential to change the way that teachers teach and children learn. In 1998, Seymour Papert gave a lecture in London entitled 'Child Power; Key to the New Learning of the Digital century'. In it, as in his book, The Connected Family, he proposed that the home and the family would be the dominant site of education and learning in the 21st Century (Papert 1996, 1998). Maybe we are just teetering on the brink of realising the ideals that futuristic educationalists led by Papert have been proposing during the last decade or more.

But wait one moment more before reaching to that limit in the sky. Will teachers become redundant in the wake of all these resources? Teachers will undoubtedly need constantly to change their ways of working and these changes may at times be measured in a single year rather than a decade as in previous times. The boundaries might certainly become infinite. But who would want to disagree with Grey: 'They will still need us (teachers) to share the learning moment, to mediate the experience, to reassure them if things go wrong, to share the next path to take. If ICT helps us dispose of the baggage but enjoy the journey it will be worthwhile. The Internet is only the start of the journey, where minds are expanded by virtual experience which in turn will lead to real experience and real learning. As always our job as teachers is to introduce it, lead them a little along the road, then set them free'. (Grey 2001).

Good teaching (in whatever mode) will always be the strongest link to pupil learning. The resources might be 'out there' readily available on-line to enhance both teaching and learning, but cyberspace has not taken over (yet).

Acknowledgement

This chapter has made extensive use of the NRICH web site. I would like to acknowledge the contribution of the NRICH project directors Toni Beardon (1996 – 2001) and Jennifer Piggott (2001 -) and all who have been connected with NRICH during its life. It is due to the team's daily work of maintaining a vibrant and ever changing web site that I have been able to write this chapter.

References

Ager, R.(2000) *The Art of Information and Communications Technology for Teachers*. David Fulton Publishers London (p 44)

Beardon, T., Jared, L., & Way, J., (1999) Mathematical Enrichment for Gifted Students – NRICH, the Online Maths Club. *Australasian Journal of Gifted Children* 8 (3). University of Melbourne

BECTa (1998) *Connecting schools, networking people*. BECTa publication.

Bentley, T. (1998) *Learning beyond the Classroom: education for a changing world*. Routledge, London

DfEE (1997) *Connecting the Learning Society - Government Consultation Document*. DfEE Publication

DfES (2002) Survey of Information & Communications Technology in Schools, England. DfES Publication

DfES (2001) *Curriculum Online* - Government Consultation Document. DfES Publication

Freeman, J. (1998), *Educating the Very Able: current international research*. HMSO London

Furlong, J., Furlong, R., Facer, K. & Sutherland, R. (2000) The National Grid for Learning: a curriculum without walls? *Cambridge Journal of Education* 30 (1). International Periodical Publishers, Oxford

Grey, D. (1999) *The Internet in School*. Cassell Education London.

Hoyles C., & Healy, L. as reported in TES 13.3 98 'Prove it'

Jared, L. (1998) NRICH evaluation report 1997-8 (NRICH internal report)

NCET (1995) *Highways for Learning*. NCET (now BECTa) publication

Papert, S. (1996) *The Connected Family: Bridging the Generation Gap*. Longstreet Press, Atlanta

Papert, S. (1998) Colin Cherry Memorial Lecture held on June 2nd 1998 at Imperial College London

Potter, J., & Mellar, H., (2000), Identifying Teachers' Internet Training Needs. *Journal of Information Technology for Teacher Education*. 9 (1). Triangle Publications, Oxford

Using role-play activity with synchronous CMC to encourage critical reflection on peer debate

Rachel Pilkington and Peter Kuminek

possible link to new view of ICT

Introduction

Putting thoughts into words is difficult. We don't always know what we think until we reflect on what we say. In this sense, describing and explaining our thoughts to others can be a form of 'acting out' our thinking which, in line with constructivist theories of experiential learning, can cause us to re-evaluate and change our conceptions. Sharing our thoughts with others allows them to comment on our thinking; dialogue exposes us to new perspectives and alternatives that can also change what we think. In Higher Education there is a need to learn to think critically and also to learn to benefit from, and contribute to, a reflective community committed to lifelong learning. As the student / tutor ratio increases there is pressure upon opportunities for students to develop these skills and a 'sense of belonging' through participation in tutor-led small-group discussions. Moreover, for some students, even when group size is small, the prospect of engaging in critical debate with tutor and fellow students can be daunting. Helping students gain confidence and motivation to develop critical thinking through debate can be difficult. Synchronous Computer Mediated Communication (CMC) might be able to play a special role here. However, learning to participate in or facilitate dialogue through CMC also presents problems. Previous work suggests that although students may be adept users of communication technologies (e.g. using online public chat rooms to manage social networks), setting up a chat room or discussion board to support a course does not guarantee students will use these tools to meet the course aims. In particular, students need to:

- understand the purpose of the discussion and how it relates to the course objectives;
- gain familiarity and confidence with relevant content material for discussion;
- gain familiarity and confidence with the genre of discussion (e.g. debate, problem-solving, co-counselling);
- gain familiarity and confidence with the tools through which discussion is mediated and learn which tool to use for which type of communication.

Tutors should take a strong, supportive and facilitating role. This chapter reports a teaching case study in which the tutor encouraged students to reflect on their participation in CMC debates through role-play activity aimed at raising student awareness of the purposes of discussion and reflecting on ways to improve the group's learning through the roles students take in the discussion. Results indicated that when supported by explicit instruction to focus on their role students felt their dialogue was better focused, more inclusive and more effective.

Perspectives on learning and the role of technology

Developmental theories of learning suggest learning is an active process of constructing representations of the world from our own experiences and through the sharing and debating of such experience with others (Piaget, 1959; Vygotsky, 1978; Cole & Wertsche, 1996). The rationale behind the design of active and constructive authentic learning tasks is that such tasks are believed to be more effective in helping students develop practical and intellectual skills and enabling conceptual understanding to be applied more appropriately in new situations. The emphasis is on students doing what we want them to be able to do, under the apprenticeship of more experienced peers or tutors (Brown, Collins & Duigard, 1989). Related perspectives include Kolb's experiential learning theory (Kolb, 1984), where the learner is engaged in a reflective cycle: acquiring new knowledge, articulating this with peers and tutor to gain a deeper understanding, attempting to apply it in practical situations and reflecting on outcomes through processes of self- and group assessment. It is hoped that students become more self-reflective practitioners, initiated into their community's vocabulary, and encouraged to see themselves as negotiators of best-practice (Wenger, 1998).

The central role of language in collaborative learning

Collaborative discussion is thought to be most effective when exposing learners to alternative perspectives and encouraging them to explain and justify their reasoning. However, effective collaboration is rarely spontaneous and must be learnt through exposure to appropriate role models and practice within a discourse community (Crook, 1994; Harwood, 1995; Robertson, Good & Pain, 1998; Wegerif & Mercer, 1996). Adult learners also require learning opportunities to develop argumentation skills (Kuhn, 1991).

In the SLANT (Spoken Language and New Technology) project primary school children were encouraged to work in small collaborative groups and make their joint reasoning explicit (Wegerif & Mercer 1996). From analysis of children's performance and dialogue protocols, children were observed using three types of talk termed disputational, cumulative and exploratory talk:

    • **disputational talk** is characterised by disagreement and individualised decision-making. There are few attempts to pool resources or offer constructive criticisms. This type of talk typically consists of short assertions, challenges and counter-assertions.

    • In **cumulative talk** participants build positively but uncritically on each other's statements and discourse often consists of repetitions, confirmations and elaborations.

• In **exploratory talk** partners engage critically but constructively with each other's ideas. Statements and suggestions offered for joint consideration may be challenged and counter-challenged, but challenges are justified, assertions are supported and alternative hypotheses offered (Wegerif & Mercer 1996, p.5).

Mercer, Wegerif & Dawes (1999) found children taught to engage in exploratory talk improved their group reasoning, and learnt to talk in an exploratory style across educational contexts.

Establishing and maintaining a discourse community

A discourse community is a social network of participants with a degree of relevant expertise, who share some set of communicative purposes and mechanisms to provide information and feedback (Swales, 1990, p.24-27). Similarly, Wenger (1998) defines a community of practice as consisting of people negotiating the division of labour toward a common goal using shared or common resources. Creating a healthy discourse community depends on tutors establishing, reinforcing and maintaining appropriate ground rules for discussion to enable these processes. Thus, it is first necessary to establish a 'safe space' in which everyone's participation is encouraged and validated. If such conditions are not met then challenges lead to disputation and some students will either not participate or engage in cumulative talk with an exclusive inner friendship group (Pilkington & Walker, in press). Wegerif and Mercer (1996, p.12) suggest the following ground rules:
- everyone should have a chance to talk;
- everyone's ideas should be carefully considered;
- each member of the group should be asked;
    o What do you think?
    o Why do you think that?
- and look and listen to the person talking;
- after discussion the group should agree on a group idea.

Berzsenyi (1999) also argues for teaching students strategies sensitive to relationships between participants. These community-building roles include actively discouraging disruptive off-task behaviour or non-constructive criticism and encouraging equal and balanced participation by inviting the views of non-contributors. Positive feedback should be given in response to useful contributions. Veerman, Andriessen and Kanselaar (2000) argue for teaching students strategies to structure/focus debate on task goals. Veerman et al. (2000) also suggest students should be encouraged to actively challenge points of view during discussion, ask for reasons and explanations or suggest counter arguments, refocus on the issue when discussion is diverted off-task and elaborate or explain ideas. Veerman et al. further suggest that CMC offers positive opportunities for developing these skills.

Computer Mediated Communication

Sotillo (2000) reported that asynchronous and synchronous CMC have different discourse features that may be exploited for different teaching and learning purposes. Asynchronous communication can give students experience closer to producing and reviewing written work than engaging in discussion. The attraction of synchronous CMC chat is that it more closely resembles real-time dialogue whilst maintaining the advantages of creating a written record that can be reviewed. CMC also allows students more opportunities to speak than traditional classrooms where the tutor tends to dominate. This can be particularly true for disadvantaged or shy students (Sullivan & Pratt, 1996; Warschauer, 1996; Veerman et al. 2000). These advantages stem partly from an apparent 'disadvantage': the violation of normal turn-taking caused by being unable to 'see' or 'hear' other participants in the process of 'speaking' (Herring, 1999). Whilst it is then more difficult to establish the ground rule 'look and listen to the person talking', it is easier to establish the rule 'everyone should have a chance to speak'. CMC often shows a lack of turn-adjacency resulting in multiple parallel threads of conversation. So users may have difficulties in keeping track of the dialogue focus. Despite this, the popularity of CMC continues to grow. Herring (1999) proposes two explanations. Firstly, the advantage of heightened interactivity means the medium still finds a useful niche amongst other genres. Secondly, users innovate alternative methods of negotiating turn-taking. Such adaptations are, however, only acquired through significant practice in using the medium.

The teaching context

The twelve-week course module 'Language, Cognition and Collaborative Learning with Computers' is an elective course for Psychology and Cognitive Science undergraduates. It aims to develop an understanding of 'how the study of language relates to the study of thinking and reasoning with particular emphasis on the changing patterns and roles of communication in learning that accompany the use of new technologies'. The module uses Communication and Information Technologies (C&IT) to provide flexible learning support and illustrate course concepts using exercises within a WebCT[1] Virtual Learning Environment (VLE). There are 22 face-to-face classroom hours (in 11 two-hour sessions) plus an 'on-call' revision session in week 12. One tutor and one demonstrator taught the module with 7 students. In odd-numbered weeks a new course topic was introduced through a short PowerPoint lecture and discussion, followed by 40 minutes of small-group practical exercises (often computer-based). Fuller Web-based course notes incorporating material in the slides and containing links to secondary Web resources were available online after each new topic, and students were asked to read these and a 'seminar paper' as preparation for sessions in even numbered weeks. In weeks with no lecture, students took part in face-to-face small group discussion activities based on the set reading and facilitated by the tutor. This was followed by practical work (often involving online discussion or other computer-based work). The strength of the approach lies in deeper student engagement as a result of having to be active and participate. However, the approach relies on students attending regularly (to complete work that extends over more than one week) and completing their preparation. It can be difficult for students used to lecture-based teaching to realise the importance of both attendance and preparation. Students can also initially worry that they are 'missing out' on content material. Some reassurance came from knowing that the online material was fuller and more flexibly

72

available than the PowerPoint lecture. Nevertheless, session plans had to have a degree of flexibility built into them. The balance between teacher-led review (using slides) and interactive discussion was partly determined by the extent to which students needed concepts from the previous session to be explained/reviewed.

The Sessions

Two face-to-face active learning sessions indicated links between two of the course topics. The first related to the advantages and disadvantages of CMC in supporting discourse communities. The second related to the value of collaborative interaction and the roles we need to play in dialogue to promote successful collaboration. This linkage of the two topics enabled students to experience some advantages and disadvantages of CMC communication themselves and helped make concrete some of the frequently discussed features of CMC described in the literature such as 'multiple parallel threads of conversation'. After that students should:

- be able to form an opinion on how these features affect communication positively and negatively and to comment critically on these features;
- experience how the adoption of various roles impacts on the quality of debate and so form an opinion on research suggesting the value of such roles for learning;
- evaluate their own chat debate, reflect on the extent to which they and other group members successfully carried out their roles and begin to recognise and adopt more effective ways of communicating using CMC.

These sessions were to take place after students had experienced WebCT synchronous chat and asynchronous discussion board. The planned sessions were designed so students would:

- discuss advantages and disadvantages of synchronous chat discussion;
- suggest ways of overcoming disadvantages of chat to improve discussion;
- role-play some strategies in a chat discussion for themselves;
- reflect on their performance and any difference in the effectiveness of the discussion as a result of the role-playing activity.

Running the Sessions

Session A – Interactive discussion on issues in using CMC

Students were asked to read beforehand Web-based notes and a seminar paper (Sullivan and Pratt, 1996). The notes contained material on writing as social action, discourse communities and features of discourse mediated by CMC tools. Six students attended and one student logged in to WebCT from home later in the session but did not take part in the exercise. Following an introduction/reminder of the topic and the set reading, the issues for discussion were elicited by asking the students to think of some of the advantages and disadvantages they had experienced using the chat tool in week two. These were summarised and re-expressed in the vocabulary of the literature as they were suggested, and written down on the whiteboard. For example if a student suggested that 'the debate was confusing because everyone was talking at once', this might have been further elaborated by saying 'yes, it can be difficult to maintain focus, the debate can lose coherence can't it? Do you remember what Herring called this feature of chat?' Someone might say 'multiple parallel threads of conversation'. This went on the whiteboard as a potential disadvantage of CMC resulting in loss of focus/coherence. On the other hand, if someone said 'it gives you time to think more about the task so you say something more relevant' then that might go down as 'time to reflect', an advantage of 'response lag' which can increase focus. The key advantages and disadvantages were thus elicited and some ways of overcoming disadvantages were suggested. Students were then given the exercise handout, including a list of issues in the form of questions to discuss (see figure 1).

Issues for Discussion

- Focus and Coherence - why might CMC increase focus in debate and why might problems in using CMC interfere with developing a focused and coherent discussion?
- Participation – who is likely to participate the most and what is the relative balance of participation likely to be in CMC vs. face-to-face (F2F) discussion?
- Personal quality – does CMC lack warmth? Is this a problem in building a discourse community?
- Constructive feedback – why might CMC increase constructive feedback in discussion and is destructive feedback equally likely?
- Advantages and disadvantages of limited bandwidth – the fact that text-based CMC lacks non-verbal and visual cues, inflection and similar audio cues to emotional content is considered a disadvantage. Why?
- Why might this restriction of bandwidth sometimes act in favour of CMC over F2F debate?

Figure 1: Issues for discussion

Students were to use the WebCT chat tool to discuss these issues in the practical part of the session. Before this the tutor initiated a discussion concerning the roles students would need to take in the discussion. Students proposed the following:
- making suggestions;
- explaining;
- asking for reasons and evidence;
- encouraging quiet students to join in by asking them what they thought;
- focusing the group on the task;
- keeping time;
- making sure there was good 'netiquette'.

These roles were written on the whiteboard as students suggested them. Every group member was to try to play these roles and, additionally, the tutor would hand each of them a secret role, an additional special responsibility in the chat. Students were not to tell anyone else what their role was but to particularly try to play this role. They were given a folded, hand-written piece of paper including the description of their secret role. The tutor's list of roles was based on both community building roles and content management roles. Community building roles were based on Berzsenyi (1999) and Johnson & Johnson (1995) whilst content and task management roles were based on Wegerif & Mercer (1996), Veerman, Andriessen & Kanselaar (2000) and Johnson & Johnson (1995). These roles related to maintaining focus on task and promoting development of argumentation skills indicative of exploratory style talk. See figure 2.

Role Name	Role
Task Management Focus	Your role is to keep people focused on the issues to be discussed, encourage them to 'move on' when necessary and discuss as many issues as possible in the time available. When people go 'off topic' remind them of the discussion issue.
Content Building	
Challenge	Your role is to challenge constructively by highlighting alternative points of view if an idea seems 'overstated' or an oversimplification. You also need to ask others to give reasons and explanations when you disagree with something someone has said.
Elaborate/Explain	Your role is to try to encourage deeper exploration of ideas. Ask others to elaborate and explain/clarify anything that is unclear or ambiguous or not explained in sufficient depth for everyone to understand.
Community Building	
Netiquette Police	Your role is to challenge any non-netiquette behaviour, e.g. overly long turns that scroll off-screen, 'flaming', bad language or disruptive behaviour such as SHOUTING or non-constructive criticism!
Balance of Participation	Your role is to work out who is participating too little and who is participating too much and then to encourage 'gently' those who are not participating to join in more e.g.: '<name> what do you think about x?'
Encourage through feedback	Your role is to provide positive feedback and encourage participation. Whenever you see a good idea well expressed try rewarding this by making sure that person knows you thought it was good, especially if that person hasn't participated before.

Figure 2: Roles given to students.

A high degree of overlap exists between roles suggested by the students and the pre-prepared secret role descriptions given by the tutor. The 'focus' role combines the suggested roles of keeping the group on task and timekeeping. However, the roles of suggesting and explaining were combined under an inquiry role in which the player asks others to elaborate/explain rather than elaborating/explaining him or herself. Explaining and elaborating is dependent on knowledge and the aim of the tutor-devised roles was to give students a chance to practise facilitating discussion whatever their level of topic knowledge. The tutor also added an additional 'encouraging role' to give positive feedback in response to good contributions.

Using issues listed in figure 1 as the chat focus, students entered the WebCT chat room to cover as many issues as possible in 40 minutes. After the chat students went to the WebCT discussion board (asynchronous CMC) and posted their impressions of using the chat tool under a prepared topic, without saying what their secret role was. Students were informed that a version of the chat discussion transcript with real names changed to pseudonyms would be reviewed later on as a group exercise and the class would try to discover who played what roles whether spontaneously or as 'secret roles'.

Session B – Reflecting on the value of adopting roles in discussion

Four students attended session B. One student previously absent analysed the transcript together with three students who attended both sessions. Three students absent from session B took part in the session A chat and recorded their impressions on the online asynchronous discussion board. Their data are included.

The tutor gave an initial resume of issues using supporting slides, leading to a discussion of the seminar paper (Wegerif and Mercer, 1996), related to the chat roles students adopted in session A. A handout listed the roles students had been given. Students were asked to identify which roles related to content building and which to task management or community building. Students grouped the roles as in figure 2. They were then given an anonymised version of the chat transcript and asked to go through it (working as a group), and allocate roles (if any) to turns, marking these against each pseudonym in the table. If a turn functioned as more than one role they should record both roles. Pseudonyms were used to make discussion less inhibiting since discussing individuals would be indirect (although, clearly, participating students might remember who had contributed what to the discussion). Totals were passed to the tutor after students had completed the activity and entered into a table on the whiteboard (figure 3). The group considered the totals and evaluated the quality of debate as a whole, plus the balance of the roles of individual students within it.

This involved students in extensive debate about which roles might have been spontaneously adopted since some individuals had more than one 'peak' role. The pseudonym (though not the real identity) of the role player given that role was revealed. An open discussion followed about how the adoption of roles had affected the overall quality of the chat and whether the chat was generally 'exploratory' in style and inclusive and encouraging of participation. The tutor referred to individual students' reflections previously reported on the asynchronous discussion board, for example: 'some of you commented on the asynchronous discussion board that you found the roles helpful – why was that?' A portion of the chat transcript appears in the appendix.

Results and Discussion

Outcome of Classroom Discussion in Session B

Student's Role Analysis During Session B							
	Role 1	Role 2	Role 3	Role 4	Role 5	Role 6	
Student alias and assigned secret role	Challenge	Elaborate/ Explain	Focus	Balance Particip- ation	Encourage	Netiquette Police	Total
Rosey (Focus)	0	0	10*	1	1	0	12
Chris (Challenge)	1	4	3	0	1	0	9
Dave (Encourage)	0	7	3	1	4	0	15
Tony (Netiquette)	0	0	2	0	0	4*	6
Cathy (Balance)	1	0	2	2*	0	1	6
Nick (Elaborate)	1	2	0	0	1	0	4
Sarah (No role, absent)							
	3	13	20	4	7	5	52
*correctly identified secret role							

Figure 3: Students' own analysis of roles taken during session B

The group successfully identified three secret roles by looking at who produced most comments judged to be a particular role. It was not always obvious. For example, Dave seemed a natural 'inquirer' asking questions such as, 'but what about lurkers?' and 'is CMC good for interaction?' Dave also did more 'encouraging' (his assigned role) by making comments such as 'that's an interesting point Nick' but the group thought his likely assigned role was elaborate/explain. There was no obvious candidate for the role 'challenger' who asked for reasons or evidence.

Overall, students viewed the chat as interesting and constructive. The group agreed that adopting roles had made this chat more focused than earlier ones. Dave commented on the bulletin board, 'I found the roles did help focus the discussion and there was less need for a supervisory figure as each person used their role to steer the conversation'. Tony also commented in online discussion that the chat was 'pretty constructive, and I aimed to address as many points as I could'. Others agreed that adopting roles meant there was more encouragement and positive feedback than in previous chats. However, Tony also commented on how concentrating on a given role might make dialogue a little artificial, looking for chances to encourage rather than naturally encouraging someone. The need to play community-building roles might conflict with contributing to building content. On the asynchronous discussion board Tony, who had the role of 'netiquette police' commented, 'my secret role meant that I was slightly preoccupied with another task'.

Cathy said it was hard to type and follow discussion at the same time; the conversation had often moved on by the time a turn was taken and this affected focus.

Chris commented: 'Clearly the chat experience highlighted the problems of turn taking. There is an obvious necessity for turn taking protocols'. In the chat, he suggested the chat tool could itself control this by disabling the keyboard of all other students once one student began talking. He also said on the asynchronous discussion board that after 'the initial novelty of engaging in chat diminished it is likely that the discussion would have become more focused'.

Several students commented that challenging was low with scope for improvement. The group agreed that challenging others to give explanations or justify their point of view was an important skill. Nick commented on the asynchronous discussion board that the chat was 'a demonstration as to the advantages and disadvantages of CMC from 1st hand experience'. This suggests that overall role play was successful in meeting its main objectives: making features of chat concrete and causing students to reflect on the quality of their own chat and the value of adopting facilitating roles within it.

Balance of Participation

Cathy, Nick and Tony took part fully in both sessions. Chris, Dave and Rosey were present in session A but absent in session B. Although this means they did not take part in the analysis of roles activity they recorded their reflections on the asynchronous discussion board.

Chris and Dave (see figure 4) contributed proportionally more than the other participants who each contributed between 12% and 16% of turns. The balance of participation was relatively good with no one person dominating. Tony commented on the asynchronous discussions board, 'compared to the F2F [face-to-face] seminar, there was considerably larger participation of all students in the CMC discussions'. The group noted that as individuals they got to say what they wanted to say, something they felt wouldn't necessarily occur in F2F discussion, and had more time to compose this so each input was more reflective. Cathy commented, 'participation was easier because you could finish your point'. Rosey said, 'personally, I definitely said more in the chat discussion than I would have in F2F discussion because in F2F you always get people who seem to dominate and take over so it's more difficult to step in and challenge them than it is on CMC'. She pointed out that 'if you are not a very confident person, or someone who gets anxious with public speaking CMC gives you the opportunity to contribute without embarrassment'. Rosey rarely contributed in F2F discussions and, as figure 4 indicates, adopting CMC was successful in encouraging her to contribute more freely.

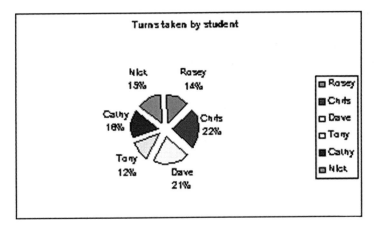

Figure 4: Balance of participation in dialogue

To further examine the effectiveness of the role-taking exercise the balance of role taking across dialogue and by student (based on the students' analysis) is examined and discussed in more detail below. See figures 5-7.

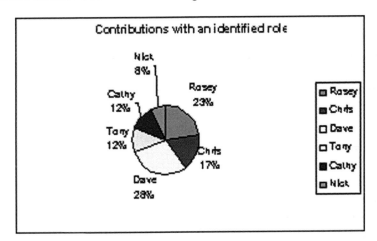

Figure 5: Contributions by student with an identified role

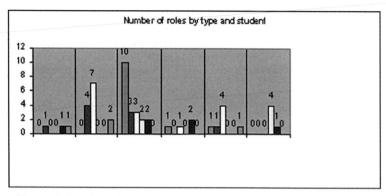

Figure 6: Breakdown of identified roles by student

Figures 5 and 6, showing turns with an identified role, illustrate that students were active in adopting their secret roles although it was not always the most frequently adopted role. This depended on how appropriate and relevant a contribution of a particular type would be, and opportunities to use some roles might have been more limited than others. Rosey and Tony stand out as having identified with their roles. Tony has more 'netiquette' management comments than other kinds. These included remarks such as 'stop being sarcastic' and 'I'm going to give Chris and Nick a warning'. Considering the balance of roles overall (see figure 7), the group as a whole were far more likely to take the role of re-focusing the chat and asking for elaborations/explanations than they were to play other roles. The role of constructively challenging was particularly infrequent. The inquiry role of elaborate/explain was used to ask for reasons. Possibly, the high number of instances of taking the focus role (not just by Rosey who was given the role, but also by others) reflects the fact that achieving focus in this medium presented difficulties.

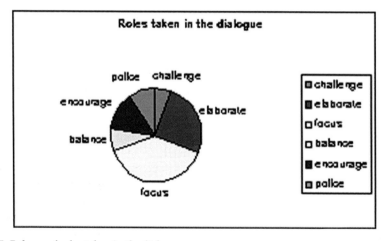

Figure 7: Balance of roles taken in the dialogue.

Focus of the discussion

The group in class and on the asynchronous discussion board noted how chat could easily lose focus owing to multiple parallel threads of conversation. Chris commented that 'clearly the chat experience highlights the problems of turn taking' and Dave that the 'chat was easily distracted'. The group also felt that adopting roles increased the focus of the discussion. Dave stated, 'the fact that the discussion was more focused than in week 2 meant that everyone was able to contribute and it seemed to be less 'private' conversations'. This further suggests greater inclusivity.

Rosey, with the focus 'secret role', was one of the least likely to contribute in face-to-face interaction. Straight away, in the chat she began 'right we've got 40 minutes so we should spend about 10 minutes on each topic and move on'. Just over 10 minutes later she followed with 'should we move on to personal quality now?' She clearly took her role seriously. On the discussion board she commented that 'the discussion was fairly focused … but I think that we did get side-tracked quite often' and 'we are all quite new to chat and it is more liberating than F2F discussion because you get time to think so you don't say something stupid'. This suggests improved quality of contribution.

Summary and Further Work

The aim in this teaching case study was to develop structured activities based on a role-playing discussion activity with a view to generating reflection on the properties of CMC. The adoption of roles in these activities seems to have been productive. Although interpretation of sessions is limited by the few students involved, they could play their roles effectively and reflect upon their part in the communication. Students engaged with the task, discussions were lively and interesting and the key concepts from the course notes appeared to be experienced directly by students, reinforcing their understanding. This exercise probably came at an ideal time; after initial familiarisation with tools and concepts, they were ready to test ideas in practice and reflect on their own performance. The analysis of chat by students in the chat gave both students and tutor an idea of how well they managed their roles. It also showed there was still some way to go in developing 'exploratory talk' through challenging each other to give reasons and evidence.

Initial results were encouraging, indicating that when supported by explicit instruction to focus on their role, students felt their dialogue was more inclusive and focused on task. At least one student indicated they would like to continue practising chat and experimenting with roles. The production of meaningful on-task discussion with no tutor participation may be considered an achievement when considering the potential of the approach for flexible and distance learning support. The applicability of the approach to other contexts and age groups is being explored. In particular, a longer programme is attempting to assist the tutor in motivating children aged nine to fourteen to develop argumentation skills (Kuminek & Pilkington, 2001). In this project more detailed coaching of strategies associated with role descriptions is explored alongside development of computer-based tools and strategies to assist tutors in scaffolding students toward the independent adoption of roles.

References

Brown, J. S., Collins, A., & Duigard, P. (1989). Situated cognition and the culture of learning. *Educational Researcher*, 1, 32-41

Berzsenyi, C. A. (1999). Teaching interlocutor relationships in electronic classrooms. *Computers and Composition*, 16, 229-246

Crook, C. (1994). *Computers and the Collaborative Experience of Learning*. London: Routledge

Cole, M., & Wertsche, J. V. (1996). Beyond the individual - social antimony in discussions of Piaget and Vygotsky. *Human development*, 34 (5), 250-256

Harwood, D. (1995). The pedagogy of the world studies 8-13 project: the influence of the presence/absence of the teacher upon primary children's collaborative group work. *British Educational Research Journal*, 21(5), 587-609

Herring, S. (1999). Interactional coherence in CMC. *Journal of Computer-Mediated Communication*, 4 (4). URL at: http://www.ascusc.org/jcmc/vol4/issue4/herring.html 11/12/01

Johnson, D. W., & Johnson, R. T. (1994). *Learning Together and Alone*. Englewood Cliffs, New Jersey: Prentice Hall

Kuhn, D. (1991). *The Skills of Argument*. Cambridge & New York: Cambridge University Press

Kuminek, P. A., & Pilkington, R. M. (2001). Helping the tutor facilitate debate to improve literacy using CMC. *Proceedings of IEEE International Conference on Advanced Learning Technologies (ICALT 2001)*, Madison, USA. 6-8th August

Kolb, D. A. (1984). *Experiential Learning: Experience as the Source of Learning and Development*. Englewood Cliffs, NJ: Prentice-Hall

Mercer, N., Wegerif, R. and Dawes, L. (1999). Children's talk and the development of reasoning in the classroom. *British Educational Research Journal*, 25 (1) 95-111

Piaget, J. (1959). *The Language and Thought of the Child* (Marjorie and Ruth Gabain, Trans.). London & New York: Routledge

Pilkington , R., & Walker, A. (in press). Using CMC to Develop Argumentation Skills in Children with a Literacy Deficit. In J. Adriessen, M. Baker, & D. Suthers (Eds.), *Arguing to Learn: Confronting Cognitions in Computer-Supported Collaborative Learning Environments*. Amsterdam: Kluwer Academic

Robertson, J., Good, J., & Pain, H. (1998). BetterBlether: The design and evaluation of a discussion tool for education. *International Journal of Artificial Intelligence in Education*, 9, 219-236

Sotillo, S. M. (2000). Discourse functions and syntactic complexity in synchronous and asynchronous communication. *Language, Learning and Technology*, 4 (1), 82-119

Sullivan, N. & Pratt E. (1996). A comparative study of two ESL writing environments: A computer-assisted classroom and a traditional oral classroom. *System*, 29 (4), 491-501

Swales, J. M. (. 1990.). *Genre Analysis: English in Academic and Research Settings*. Cambridge: Cambridge University Press

Vygotsky, L. S. (1978). *Mind in Society: The Development of Higher Psychological Processes*. Cambridge, Mass: Harvard University Press

Warschauer, M. (1996). Comparing Face-to-Face and Electronic Discussion in the Second Language Classroom. *CALICO Journal*, 13, 7-26

Wegerif, R., & Mercer, N. (1996). Computers and reasoning through talk in the classroom. *Language and Education*, 10 (1), 47-64

Wenger , E. (1998). *Communities of Practice: Learning, Meaning, and Identity*. Cambridge: Cambridge University Press

Veerman, A. L., Andriessen, J. E. B., & Kanselaar, G. (2000). Learning through synchronous electronic discussion. *Computers and Education*, 34, 269-290

Appendix – Section of Chat Transcript

An early extract from the chat in which students discuss the issue of focus (turns 51-79).

51.	Dave Edwards	Shall we discuss all the advantages first?
52.	Chris Bailey	turn taking quite clearly seems to be a problem - has anyone got any suggestions on what an appropriate mehtod might be to overcome this?
53.	Rosey King	focus maybe increases because you don't get sidetracked about other issues, well i suppose you do a little like we all are, but in a learning situation it make make for less genearl banter
54.	Cathy Underwood	ok the advantages of cmc re participantion what do you thinkgroup?
55.	Dave Edwards	if each person replies in turn?
56.	Nick Berry	I think if we discuss the disadvanatges first cos then we might be able to progress and sort them out
57.	Chris Bailey	is anyone actually conforming to their suggested roles?
58.	Tony Parker	In terms of turn taking - I think we should propse a question and then waut for everyone's response?
59.	Dave Edwards	cathy - it's better than in the classroom but what about the lurkers?
60.	Rosey King	the more people, the less participation all round and people necome dominant, what do you all think about that issue in participation?
61.	Cathy Underwood	chris, i agree, what do the rest of the group think
62.	Dave Edwards	what is necome?
63.	Rosey King	become
64.	Chris Bailey	you agrre about what?
65.	Dave Edwards	what is agrre?
66.	Chris Bailey	someone pose the question?
67.	Dave Edwards	let's all concentrate on our spelling!!
68.	Tony Parker	dave I think we shouldn't quibble over silly spelling mistakes - try to stay focused
69.	Cathy Underwood	what are the advs and disds of cmc re participation

70.	Nick Berry	I think that us just having problems highlights the issues pretty well, what do you think gang?
71.	Dave Edwards	that's an interesting point Nick
72.	Chris Bailey	what about a system whereby as soon as someone starts typing all the others in the chat are disabled? encouraging the chat to become more focused?
73.	Rosey King	disadv-lurkers, adv-more student contributions rather than just teacher talking
74.	Nick Berry	how do you propose to do that?
75.	Dave Edwards	but wouldn't that be a bit painful Chris?
76.	Chris Bailey	you talking to me Nick?
77.	Cathy Underwood	Nick, yes it seems that although coversation is supposedly "synchronous" the time lag and turn-taking problems makes particpation in CMC quite confusing
78.	Chris Bailey	keyboard disablement
79.	Tony Parker	I think if you look at all the particpation so far - I think you will all agree that eeryone has particpated at least 6 times more than the oral disussion earlier

[i]WebCT is a registered trademark for more information see URL: http://www.webct.com/ 15/01/02

Computers in Schools and Colleges: The User in Control

Jocelyn Wishart

With thanks to Sheila Fisher who carried out the work in school described in Research Project 3.

This chapter describes four research projects that informed our understanding of students' motivations to learn through the use of information and communications technologies (ICT). The one finding that runs throughout studies of the impact of computers on teaching and learning is the consistent reporting of students' enhanced motivation to learn. Motivation is an important pre-requisite to successful learning; the beneficial effects of increased student motivation through the use of ICT were seen to impact upon learning in curriculum subjects where ICT was used (Watson, 1993).

However, Denning (1997) pointed out in a Report on ICT and pupil motivation that inappropriate and uninformed application of ICT in classrooms may still result in poor motivation and disappointing learning outcomes. For successful curriculum development through ICT teachers and lecturers need to understand effective strategies for the use of ICT in teaching and learning. The following research projects carried out between 1996 and 2000 all point to the key factor for successful application of ICT in the curriculum as being the enabling of user control over the computer and consequent learning through it.

The first project reports teachers' and pupils' perceptions of changes in their teaching and learning following the installation of a computer network throughout a large secondary school. Changes took a year to impact upon the curriculum, with most teachers (86 % of comments) reporting changes to their teaching resulting in increased use of ICT. However, this was likely to be the use of ICT to replace an earlier method of carrying out a departmentally set task rather than a clear change of teaching style. Both pupils and teachers noted an increase in pupils' independence and use of open, flexible learning skills.

In the second project teachers and pupils from a range of secondary schools were interviewed about their use of multimedia CD-ROMs. The potential benefit of ICT for developing the curriculum through more open and flexible learning became obvious. The teachers reported strongly that having multimedia encyclopaedias on CD-ROM in school enhanced their teaching by enabling more independent, student-centred learning. The pupils noted the ease of use of CD-ROMs compared to large books and their enjoyment of the accompanying graphics and sound.

The concept of giving pupils more independence over their learning with ICT was investigated practically in the third project. Two classes of 13–14-year-old pupils carrying out a Humanities learning and assessment exercise were given a free choice as to whether and how they used technologies such as computer, video and CD-ROM to support their work. The results were impressive with two-thirds of the pupils achieving a higher grade than in their previous assessed exercise and 77% of them reporting that they preferred having the element of choice in using ICT.

Not all pupils enjoyed being given this independence. Some light is thrown as to how individuals differ in their response to being given choice over ICT use by psychological research into individual locus of control. The fourth project investigated how university students vary in approach and attitude to computer use and how this was linked to beliefs about control or lack of control of their environment and what happens to them.

Why User Control is Important to Learning with Computers

The importance of choice and autonomy to pupil learning has been justified theoretically by psychologists studying links between motivation and learning. Byrnes (1996) pointed out that students can become intrinsically motivated when they have control over their environment, set challenges for themselves and satisfy their curiosities.   He cites research by Stipek (1993) where researchers found that future competence will follow successes, particularly if students believe they controlled the success.

Byrnes discusses the role of self-efficacy, linking the agency beliefs (beliefs that enable individuals to personally control successes) proposed by Skinner et al. (1988) to the idea of intrinsic motivation. Control or choice within learning environment motivates pupils and so engenders success; this in itself leads to further motivation. Empowering students in terms of learning environment as well as imbuing feelings of self-efficacy suggests that if we explicitly indicate to students that they control their successes it will be extremely advantageous in motivating them to future successes.

Wishart (1990) investigated the effects three cognitive factors, user control, challenge and visual complexity, had on motivation to use and learning from an educational computer game. The game was intended for young children and illustrated how to get out of a house fire safely. Three hundred primary school students played different versions of the game which had been constructed to provide user control of movement through the house, challenge through scoring points and visual complexity through use of graphic effects in different combinations. Control through user choice was found to be the most significant factor in creating involvement with and learning from the software.

The work of Underwood and Underwood (1990) reinforced this view in their study of the role of computers in the learning process, emphasising that if learners were in control or in charge of their learning they responded to and appreciated their independence.

Lepper et al. (1993) summarised this cognitive approach to motivation in their proposal that an expert tutoring system should provide four major motivational goals:

to maintain the learner's sense of personal control, to enhance self-confidence, to produce an appropriate level of challenge and to elicit a high level of curiosity.

Underwood (1994) reviewed case studies looking at use of databases in classroom practice. Here much of the valued learning experiences centred on ways in which students took responsibility for learning outcomes and how new technologies could support moves to more independent approaches to learning. Davis et al. (1997) argued that the degree of autonomy pupils had over the pace and content of their learning with ICT was directly related to an increase in the quality of learning itself. Using software to provide an open learning environment encouraging student autonomy and choice is seen as good practice in ICT teaching in the United Kingdom (NCET/NAACE, 1994).

The following three examples discuss the impact of initiatives in ICT provision on the nature of independent learning tasks and pupil autonomy in teaching and learning in UK Secondary Schools.

Research Project 1: A Survey of Teachers' and Pupils' Perceptions of Changes in Teaching and Learning in a School following the Installation of a Computer Network

The study resulted from a request from school governors for a formal evaluation of the impact and use of a newly installed network. This network comprised 97 personal computers distributed around the school in large suites (15-20 PCs), small suites (5-6 PCs) or in classrooms (2 PCs per room) according to preferences expressed by individual departments. These were supported by 2 File Servers, a Multimedia 4 CD Server and the school engaged the services of a full-time network manager.

The evaluation was structured in two phases to provide an early indication of initial reactions and attitudes on the part of staff and pupils (phase 1) and a longer term view documenting changes in attitudes, modes of use and teaching and learning styles over the first full academic year of computer use (phase 2).

In phase 1, five members of the evaluation team spent one day in school talking to staff and pupils about their use of the network. This enabled the team to become familiar with the school layout, the location of network terminals, personnel in the different departments and available software. Issues were identified and separate but matching questionnaires designed for all academic staff and a stratified, random sample of pupils. Initial questionnaires were distributed to all 95 teaching staff in the school and to the pupil sample which was constructed using a random number generator to select pupils, male and female, from each tutor group making 217 pupils in all.

The initial questionnaire (phase 1) was returned by 69 members of staff and 161 pupils giving response rates of 73% and 74% respectively. Interviews with a range of members of staff followed and a second shorter questionnaire devised, to deal with issues identified during this by the evaluation team and senior management of the school. This second follow-up questionnaire was distributed to all those who took part in the initial survey, except those who were no longer available, for example the pupils from Years 11 and 13. Questionnaires were returned by 49 staff and 81 pupils making the response rates for the follow-up: 71% for staff and 73% for pupils.

In both questionnaires teachers and pupils were asked for comments in their own words on the effects the new computer network had on teaching styles and pupils' learning. A content analysis of these comments was then carried out.

Table 1 shows the results of the content analysis of teachers' answers to the question in the original survey: How has the installation of the computer network affected your teaching style?

Table 1: Changes in Teaching Style since the installation of the computer network

Effect	Total % (n=74)
Makes things more difficult	14
Little or no change	24
Changed to include ICT	19
Changed because enjoy using ICT	3
Improved lessons	16
Improved lesson preparation	7
Enables independent, open-ended work	5
Enables differentiation	12

Forty-three per cent of teachers' comments indicated that the use of ICT improved their teaching in a variety of ways though more use of independent learning tasks was rarely mentioned. The most common comment was that it had made little or no difference (24%) though a proportion (14%) noted that having to use ICT made teaching more difficult owing to a variety of physical problems such as room swaps and a fixed schedule of time in the ICT room.

By the end of the academic year more changes in their teaching style were noted in the follow-up survey (shown in table 2).

Table 2: Comments about changes in teaching style noted in follow-up survey

Comment	Total % (n=42)
now using applications software for subject-based tasks	29
increased use of ICT	24
more independent learning tasks set	17
more successful at managing ICT in lessons	14
department now directs ICT use	12
improved planning and presentation	5

Most comments (86%) reported changes to teaching resulting in increased use of ICT though this was more likely to be use of ICT to replace earlier methods of carrying out departmentally set tasks (29%) or a result of teachers being scheduled to use the

ICT room (12%) than a clear change to a less didactic teaching style (17%). Fourteen per cent of staff reported increased success in managing the use of ICT in lessons.

Pupils were asked in the follow-up survey to report changes in the way their teachers taught.

Table 3: Changes in Teaching reported by pupils in the follow-up survey

Comment	Total % (n=57)
Negative comments	7
No effect	46
Made it easier	5
Made lessons more fun/interesting	4
Made for more independent learning	11
Improved teaching	11
Increased use of ICT	14
Other comments	2

Thirty-one per cent of pupils' comments reported positive effects of the use of ICT on their teachers' teaching with more use of independent, open learning tasks highlighted. A further 14% of comments noted that use of IT has increased since the first survey but these are overshadowed by the 46% of comments still reporting no change.

Staff were asked in the follow-up survey about the impact of computers on the children's learning strategies.

Table 4: Effects upon the learning strategies adopted by pupils since the previous survey, as reported by staff

Comments about	Total % (n=67)
Wastes time	4
No effect	1
Mixed comment	4
Increased motivation	28
Increased independence and open, flexible learning skills	16
More attention to presentation and spelling	13
Increased concentration on task	7
They achieve more	4
Increased confidence	4
More logical, problem solving work and discussion	6
Use of ICT for class/homework	6
Other positive comments	3

More of the teachers' comments (90%) referred to positive effects of use of the computer network on students' learning than when first asked with only 4% referring to negative effects. The most common comment (28%) referred to increased motivation seen in students when using ICT. A significant number of comments referred to increased independent learning and research skills (16%) and pupils paying more attention to presentation of their work including spelling (13%).

Overall, the proportion of teachers' comments reporting changes to teaching style since the installation of the computer network rose over the year from 62% in the first survey to 72% in the second. There appears to be a mismatch here, as consistently half the pupils' comments reported no change in their teachers' teaching. Changes implemented by teachers were either transparent to pupils or the changes occurred in how teachers planned and thought about their teaching rather than in their behaviour.

Specific changes to teaching style were observed by both staff and pupils; one noted by both teachers and pupils in both questionnaires was the change in tasks set for pupils to more open, independent learning assignments. Simultaneously, pupils showed their appreciation of such changes, reporting that their learning was made easier and the teaching had improved.

In an open, independent learning assignment the pupil has more control over the task than one with a fixed structure dictated by the teacher. This perception of control as described by Lepper et al. (1993) and Wishart (1990) is intrinsically motivating for pupils.

The most common teachers' comment about changes in pupils' learning since the network installation reported increased motivation in lessons. The proportion of this comment rose over the year from 16% to 28% of comments made in initial and follow-up surveys. This increased motivation resulted in better work as the teachers noted pupils' increased attention to presentation (13% of comments), concentration on task (7% of comments) and greater achievement and confidence (both 4% of comments) in the follow-up survey.

The pupils' perceptions of greater control over their work were likely to be responsible for enhanced motivation but other intrinsic and extrinsic motivators such as challenge, curiosity, self-esteem, entertainment and immediate feedback were also seen to be present.

Research Project 2: Interviews with Teachers about Use of Multimedia CD-ROMS

In a different investigation of the impact of multimedia CD-ROMs on teaching and learning in UK Secondary Schools eight schools were selected to provide a representative sample of different types of school in the area: local authority-maintained high schools and colleges, direct grant-maintained and independent schools.

Twenty-six teachers and 61 pupils from 8 schools were interviewed in detail about their schools' use of multimedia CD-ROMs in teaching and learning. The observations made in these interviews were recorded and similar comments grouped together for a thematic content analysis.

When asked how having multimedia encyclopaedias on CD-ROM in school enhanced their teaching, the teachers' most common comment was that it enabled more independent, student-centred learning (15% of their responses). This can be linked to their second most common comment (13%), that CD-ROMs were more motivating for students through applying Lepper et al. (1993) recommendations and Wishart's (1990) theory of intrinsic motivation through being allowed to be in control of software and learning environment. Indeed the use of CD-ROM encyclopaedias for independent research was well recommended by Collins et al. (1997).

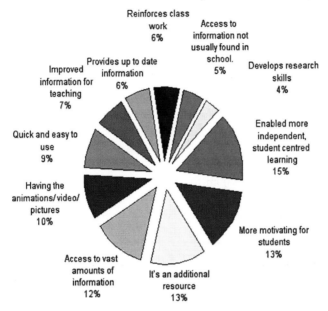

Figure 1: What is it about multimedia CD-ROMs that enhances your teaching?   *(n=82 comments from 26 teachers)*

However, when pupils were asked about what makes multimedia CD-ROM encyclopaedias better to learn from (figure 2) the most popular response was presence of graphics, video and sound (22%). Being easier to use (17%), enjoyable and fun (11%), quicker to use (9%) and being able to print off from the CD-ROM (8%) were also mentioned often.

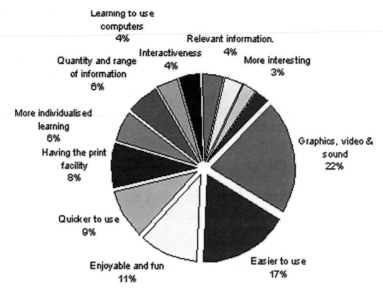

Figure 2: What is it about multimedia CD-ROMs that makes it better to learn from them? (n= 61 students, 137 comments)

When looking at differences between responses from different age groups, the presence of graphics, video and sound was the most common response for only the oldest (18% of comments) and youngest (23% of comments) age groups. It formed only 7% of comments from years 10-11 for whom the convenience of using CD-ROM was the most important (13% of comments).

The sense of being in control proposed by Wishart (1990) as motivating students to use ICT appeared only as the second most common response made by the youngest age group when asked what makes it better to learn from CD-ROMs. Freedom to explore and find things out for yourself was mentioned in 9% of comments from years 7-9.

Research project 3. Case Study: Giving Pupils Autonomy and Choice in Use of Computer Software

Whether being given control is important to learning with ICT was tested in a small research project on giving pupils autonomy and choice over their work carried out in the Humanities department of a Leicestershire High School. There were two classes involved making 61 pupils, 27 boys and 32 girls, from year 9 (13–14-year-olds). These pupils were to undertake a learning task that required the development of appropriate history skills and could be enhanced by the use of ICT in terms of accessing, handling and communicating information.

The task itself involved pupils testing the hypothesis that the Industrial Revolution was a Good Thing. It was devised to enable pupils to use primary and secondary historical sources and to interpret and analyse evidence to draw substantiated conclusions. It was also a well-established assessment unit, as part of the Year 9 History Scheme of Work. To test this hypothesis pupils could use a range of sources, video, texts, books, documents available on the Internet and CD-ROM, comparing and evaluating information to reach an appropriate conclusion. The use of ICT would extend the range of sources available and could act as a tool for both accessing information and presenting work.

To enable the fullest possible choice most appropriately the teaching groups were located in the computer room, although certain adjustments had to be made. Desks away from the computer stations were essential, a choice of software packages and printing facilities needed to be accessible and other resources placed in the room to enable access to a range of information sources. The teacher was helped in planning and organising the project in that it did not coincide with any significant ICT tasks in other curriculum areas.

After pupils completed this work, it was assessed by their teacher for level of attainment using the standards given in the UK National Curriculum for History (DfE,1995) and compared with the level obtained for their last piece of assessed work. Both groups completed the set work on time to an appropriate standard. Their use of ICT included a range of presentation and information packages far wider than used in previous assessment tasks for History that had made use of ICT.

One reason for their success was their familiarity with the available software. Pupils chose a package largely because they were familiar with it or found it easy to use. Had the pupils not had recent experience with the software it is likely the project would not have gone as well.

Overwhelmingly, 89 % of pupils reported that using computers helped them do better in their work and indeed 67% achieved a National Curriculum level better than their previous assessment. Whether this would have been achieved in a normal assessment situation is difficult to say but all pupils showed a good historical knowledge of the period studied and used in general a wider range of historical evidence, gathered from a greater number of sources than in previous tasks. Without exception the groups had concentrated to a greater degree throughout and had been better motivated than in previous assessments.

The questionnaires revealed generally very positive feelings towards the work and use of ICT. The largest proportion of pupils' explanations as to why using ICT helped was because it enabled them to present work better (31% of comments) followed by (18% of comments) it helped them work more quickly. This focus on improved presentation was also found by Cox (1997) who linked it to enhancing the pupils' sense of achievement in their learning. There were considerably fewer negative comments but printer problems were cited in 50% of them.

Table 5: Reasons given by pupils for whether ICT helped them to do better or not

Reasons given for Yes (n=101)	%
Better presentation	31
Quicker than written work	18
Helps with spelling & grammar	11
Enjoy using computers / find it more fun	9
Prefer using computers so work harder	8
Easier	8
Provided a lot of / wide range of information	7
I did not need to rewrite / make rough drafts	3
A change from the usual work	3
Being able to choose what to use and when to use it	3
Reasons for No (n=8)	%
Waiting for the printer / printer problems	50
We could have easily done it by hand	25
It slows me down	25

Clearly, for these pupils the element of choice in use of ICT had a positive effect on their approaches to work with 77% reporting that they preferred it and none saying that they disliked it. The reasons they gave are shown in table 6. They enjoyed most being able to use the software they chose when they wanted (22% of answers), not being told what to do and being able to choose not to use the computer (both 18% of answers). When given this choice they made full use of it, choosing a range of options, some familiar and some new. The pupils had some insight into what perhaps made their learning more effective, with 16% of comments reporting that having choice improved the quality of their work. The results of this study appear to support the proposals of Underwood and Underwood (1990) that learners will respond positively to being in charge of their learning through use of ICT.

Table 6: Pupils' reasoning with regard to free choice

Why it made no difference (n=2)	%
Because you still work just as hard either way	100
Why it was good (n=55)	%
I could use the software I wanted, when I wanted to.	22
It helped because I didn't have to always use the computer	18
I could work how I wanted rather than being told what to do	18
It improved the quality of my work	16
More independence to work in our own way, at our own speeds.	11
We could go and do the work at any time of the day	7
I didn't have to use a package which I do not know or like	4
It's better than ordinary work	4

The overall success of the task was pleasing, however it is worth noting that these were top sets, competent in the use of ICT and in setting up a historical investigation. The same will not be true of other groups where the range of ability will be much wider and will include pupils with special educational needs and those whose confidence and competence with ICT is limited. Such considerations will inevitably make the outcomes less clear. There is enough however in the success of this project to indicate that a similar assessment unit could be developed with less able pupils in mind.

To enable pupils to be increasingly autonomous in the use of ICT in the learning environment is an objective to be encouraged. It is important that this is established over time, as one-off sessions will not enable pupils to experience a pattern of practice that allows them to gain the experience, skills and confidence necessary to take charge of their learning and to make sensible, realistic and appropriate choices about the part ICT plays in this. This will be particularly important for pupils who are at the lower end of the ability range.

Teachers need to manage the learning environment in as flexible a way as the confines of a school allows. Certainly the availability of resources and use of space are important considerations. Computer rooms are in great demand and often do not have enough general workspace to allow more flexible use of ICT. In this instance, the organisation took much longer in time and preparation than anticipated as the area used had to be set up for the task every lesson.

This successful unit is now a designated task linking Humanities and ICT National Curriculum requirements (DfEE, 1995a and b) within the school. It also explored the way ICT can be used as part of the process of independent learning in which pupils themselves, in view of the ever increasing use of technology, can be in charge and better motivated to learn.

Research Project 4. Individual Differences in Attitudes towards being given Control of a Computer

The examples previously discussed show the importance to education professionals of understanding why pupils having a sense of control over their use of ICT is important for their learning through its use. However, in each of these studies there were some pupils who preferred not to use computers. Possibly, how prepared someone is to become involved with a computer is related to how they feel about being put in control of it (Wishart, 1998).

People differ in how much they accept that they personally control their successes (see introduction to this chapter). Being given control or choice will engender intrinsic motivation only in those who believe that they influence what happens to them as opposed to those who believe that anything that happens to them results from fate or acts by others. This continuum of belief from being internally to externally controlled was first introduced by Rotter (1966) to explain the differences between individuals in how they make attributions about their successes or failures and how this affects their learning. He named this new construct 'locus of control'.

Those who believe they influence everything that happens to them have a very internal locus of control and learn from the results of their actions whereas those who believe that anything that happens to them results from outside factors have a very external locus of control. This latter group find it difficult to learn from their actions as they do not believe their action affected the results obtained.

Other research has shown that the original concept of locus of control put forward by Rotter (1966) is not the simple continuum described above. Levenson (1972) proposed that Rotter's scale was multidimensional and in studies, both with normal subjects and psychiatric patients (1972, 1973), she found two definite dimensions: control by powerful others and control by fate or gods. She also found evidence for a possible third dimension: control by oneself. This was confirmed by Reid and Ware (1974) who measured the locus of control of 167 university students and used factor analysis to reveal the same three dimensions.

In the light of this research, Coovert and Goldstein (1980) measured American university students' positive and negative attitudes toward computers using Levenson's scale to measure their locus of control for the three dimensions. The results confirmed their hypothesis that those with positive attitudes who regard the computer as a tool to be used would score highly on internal control of oneself and low on the other two dimensions. However, their second hypothesis that those with negative attitudes would regard the computer as a powerful other and so score highly on the control by others dimension and low on the other two was not confirmed.

This leads to the hypothesis that belief in control by oneself or internal control affects attitude to and use of computers. If people believe they are in control and, as reported by Wishart (1990), being in control of a computer is rewarding, then they are happy using a computer. However, if people believe they are not in control, being placed in charge of a computer is unsettling and leads to conflicting emotions.

Should the above hypothesis be proven, then differentiated training strategies need be provided for both school pupils and university students according to how they feel about controlling computers for it has become imperative that **all** students become familiar with the use of ICT in their learning.

This hypothesis was investigated in a survey of professional trainees at universities in the UK using opportunity samples of student nurses and students in initial teacher training.

For some years now, students in teacher and nurse training have been required to make effective use of ICT in their studies and their work. In the case of teacher training the Department for Education and Employment (DfEE, 1998) has specified a National Curriculum in ICT to be followed by all teacher-training institutions. For nursing there is no similar formal requirement though the United Kingdom Central Council (UKCC, 2000) requires that before entry onto the nursing register students are able to demonstrate the computer skills needed to record, enter, store, retrieve and organise data essential for care delivery. The uses these students have previously made of computers and the attitudes they developed towards ICT will affect how they respond to the compulsory ICT training during their course.

The 154 students in nurse training and 128 students in initial teacher training were asked to report on the uses they had made of computers, their attitudes towards them and to complete a questionnaire (Duttweiler, 1984) to locate their locus of internal control. Though the groups had similar age profiles the teacher-training students were more likely than the nursing students to have access to a home computer, to use computers more often, to have used a greater variety of software applications and as a group to have a more internal locus of control (table 7).

Table 7: Differences between teacher and nurse trainees in computer use and internal locus of control

	Teacher Trainees	Nurse Trainees
% of group with access to a home computer	74%	63%
Frequency of computer use (median)	Every day	Weekly
Median number of software applications used	10	6
Median internal locus of control index	105	96

This may result from a gender effect as 45% of the teacher-training students were male compared to 17% of nursing students.

For both teacher training and nursing students having a more internal locus of control correlates slightly but significantly with more positive attitudes towards computers. For example, the overall correlation, calculated using Spearman's Rho, between internal locus of control and liking to use computers was rho = 0.3 and for between internal locus of control and being scared of using computers was rho = -0.33. Both values were statistically significant at $p<.01$.

Thus students who are less internally controlled, who believe they are less likely to influence what happens to them, are more likely to be apprehensive about using computers. It is extremely important that these students achieve positive experiences of ICT early in their course if they are to continue with its use. Tutors need to differentiate their course material according to a student's experience of and attitudes to ICT to ensure successful control of computers. Initially the tutor needs to provide students with appropriate software, applications with opportunities for user control for more internally controlled individuals and more heavily structured tasks for more externally controlled individuals.

Conclusions

The results of these four projects suggest that where teachers and lecturers are planning their teaching with ICT they should
- take note of the increased opportunity for organising independent learning tasks supported through a range of software;
- bear in mind the need to provide differentiated support material or software according to the learners' attitudes towards being given control of a computer.

The first project revealed that changes in teaching and learning following the installation of a computer network in school took a year to impact upon the curriculum. One early change to teaching style, noted by both staff and pupils, was the change in type of tasks set for the pupils to more open, independent learning assignments. The pupils showed their appreciation of such changes reporting that their learning was made easier and their teaching had improved. This change of teaching style with the introduction of ICT was confirmed in the second project. When teachers in a range of secondary schools were interviewed as to how the use of multimedia CD-ROMs enhanced their teaching their most common response was that the technology enabled more independent, student-centred learning.

In the third research project, a clear change of teaching style to give students autonomy over their work and learning through use of ICT was tested and shown to be both academically successful and popular with the students themselves. However, as shown in the fourth project described, individuals vary in both how they feel about being given control and choice over ICT use and in their previous experiences of ICT. Therefore, a variety of support mechanisms needs to be considered by the teacher or lecturer.

References

Byrnes, J. P. (1996) *Cognitive Development and Learning in Instructional Contexts*. Allyn and Bacon

Collins, J., Hammond, M. and Wellington, J. (1997) *Teaching and Learning with Multimedia*. Routledge London and New York

Coovert, M. D. and Goldstein, M. (1980) Locus of control as a predictor of users' attitude towards computers. *Psychological Reports*, 47, pp. 1167-1173

Cox, M. J. (1997) *The Effects of Information Technology on Students' Motivation*. Kings College & NCET

Davis N., Desforges, C., Jessel, J., Somekh, B., Taylor, C. and Vaughan, G. (1997) in Somekh, B. and Davis, N. (ed) (1997) *Using Information Technology Effectively in Teaching and Learning*. Routledge

Denning, T. (1997) *IT and Pupil Motivation*. Keele University/NCET

DfEE (1995a) *History in the National Curriculum*. London HMSO

DfEE (1995b) *Information Technology in the National Curriculum*. London: HMSO

DfEE (1998) *Teaching: High Status, High Standards*. Requirements for Courses of Initial Teacher Training (Circular 4/98) Annex B. DfEE, London

Duttweiler, P. C. (1984) The internal control index: a newly developed measure of locus of control. *Educational and Psychological Measurement*, 44, 209-221

Fisher, E. (1993) in Scrimshaw, P. (1993) *Language, Classrooms and Computers*, Routledge

Lepper, M. R., Woolverton, M., Mumme, D. L. and Gurtner, J. L. (1993) Motivational techniques of Expert Human Tutors: Lessons for the Design of Computer-based Tutors in Lajoie, S. P. and Derry, S. J. (eds) *Computers as Cognitive Tools*. Hillsdale: Lawrence Erlbaum Associates

Levenson, H. (1972) Distinctions within the concept of internal-external control:

Development of a new scale. *Proceedings of the 80th Annual Convention of the American Psychological Association*, 7, pp. 259-260 (Summary)

Levenson, H. (1973) Multidimensional locus of control in psychiatric patients. *Journal of Consulting and Clinical Psychology*, 41 (3), pp. 397-404

NCET/NAACE (1994) *Inspecting IT*. Coventry: NCET

Reid, D.W. and Ware, E. E. (1974) Multidimensionality of internal versus external control: addition of a third dimension and non-distinction of self versus others *Canadian Journal of Behavioural Science*, 6 (2), pp. 131-142

Rotter, J.B. (1966) Generalised expectancies for internal versus external locus of reinforcement. *Psychological Monographs*, 80 (1) (whole no. 609)

Skinner, E. and Chapman, M. and Baltes, P. (1988) Control, means-end, agency beliefs. A new conceptualisation and its measurement during childhood, *Journal of Personality and Social Psychology*, 54

Somekh, B. in Somekh, B. and Davis, N. (ed) (1997) *Using Information Technology Effectively in Teaching and Learning*. Routledge

Stipek (1993) cited in Byrnes, J. P. (1996) *Cognitive Development and Learning in Instructional Contexts*. Allyn and Bacon

UKCC (2000) *Requirements for pre-registration nursing programmes*. Available from http://www.ukcc.org.uk/cms/content/publications/default.asp?pg=5 [Last accessed 12.01.01]

Underwood, J. and Underwood, G. (1990) *Computers and Learning*, Blackwell

Underwood, J. (ed) (1994) *Computer based learning: Potential into Practice*, David Fulton

Watson, D. (1993) *The Impact Report*. London: Department for Education and King's College

Wishart, J. (1990) Cognitive factors related to user involvement with computers and their effects upon learning from an educational computer game, *Computers and Education*, Vol 15 (1-3), 145-150

Wishart, J. (1998) Initial Teacher Training Students' Attitudes to use of IT and Individual Locus of Control. *Journal of Information Technology for Teacher Education*, 6 (3), 271-284

ICT and curriculum provision in early years

Deirdre Cook

Biological computers

Readers of the book *How babies think* (Gopnick et al., 1999) are asked to consider an interesting metaphor, babies or young children as sophisticated biological computers capable of working on coded input to increasingly make sense of the world around them. The authors outline how knowing more about thinking and learning has helped scientists to construct ever more powerful computers but unlike the computers we use, young children:

> ... can change their own programs. They have emotions and drives that actively cause them to explore the world and learn more. And they get information from other people who are in fact, designed to fulfil just this purpose.
>
> (p. 172)

The important ideas embedded here and the image the metaphor offers us are far from frivolous. Many key features of young children's learning are similar to those connected with ICT: self direction, the drive to explore, find things out, make sense of experiences in an increasingly complex way and perhaps most importantly of all, use other people when they need information or help.

Beliefs, values and principles

The early childhood tradition places high value upon multi-sensory, active, first-hand experiences for young children and emphasises the quality of interactions between young learners and their environment and also those taking place between them and adults and other children they encounter. While educators may find one theory or model of learning more convincing than another, there is widespread consensus about the qualities young children bring to learning and that it is the adult's responsibility to capitalise on these supportively. A wide consensus exists also about the centrality of play and the significance of its contribution to all areas of development. It is important to reaffirm these beliefs when considering the place of ICT in the early childhood curriculum.

One response to safeguarding traditional notions of childhood is to close our eyes to technological changes. However, the telecommunications industry ensures that consumers, old and young, are well aware of all the potential on offer. Anecdotes about young children's prowess, at increasingly early ages, with timers, control devices, phones, videos and many other devices intended for adult users are legion. Educational publications suggest that as these devices become more commonplace, and more user-friendly, their use by young children at home will increase. A USA industry consumer report suggested that early education was the biggest growth area for software, claiming that 70% of people with young children and a home computer had purchased learning materials (SPA Consumer Market Report, 1996). A more recent study looking at popular culture and literacy showed in the research family diaries of three- and four-year-olds evidence of activity with computer games, with only four out of eighteen families not having either a games console or a PC. (Marsh and Thompson, 2001)

The anxieties of carers and educators deserve to be treated seriously and include concerns for children's social and emotional well-being, their physical health, the shortening or even demise of childhood, and possible neglect of cognitive development. The nightmare scenario of helping to create anti-social, uncommunicative, screen-obsessed zappers is truly frightening. The reality, happily, is somewhat different. Like any other resource, computers need to be used in ways appropriate for children's stages of development. Papert (1996) says that to ask how old children should be to use computers is rather like asking when they should have crayons or dolls. He is quite clear that just as computers can be well used at any age, so too can they be badly used. He states:

> I am fearful of using computers as 'baby stimulators' and 'baby-sitters' by exploiting their holding power before we understand it enough to use it wisely. I am fearful of the idea that children can be better prepared for life by doing schoolish kinds of learning at the earliest possible age. [.....]To these old objections I add a new one: The computer opens opportunities for new forms of learning that are far more consistent with the nature of the young child. How absurd then to use it to impose old forms.
>
> (pp.98-99)

Young Children's learning and the curriculum

The idea that 'new forms of learning' associated with ICT might conflict with older forms is particularly pertinent to early childhood education where debate surrounding the nature of the curriculum has been particularly intense. The old forms of learning Papert has in mind are not those of the great educational thinkers, such as Froebel, Montessori, Piaget, Bruner and the Macmillan sisters, who inspired generations of early childhood educators to consider the total well-being of the child as paramount. Papert is a self-identified constructivist whose view is very much in the tradition of these great educational thinkers. He believes in the power of self direction but is realistic enough to recognise that in an educational setting a certain amount of instruction offers some practical utility. He advocates paying careful attention to the 'balance' between the two approaches of construction and instruction. He feels one of the greatest dangers is that computers too easily lend themselves to the practices of the 'old forms' of the curriculum, and can tip the balance too easily towards narrow notions of basic-skills and instruction.

The 'curriculum debate' is summed up by Anning and Edwards who claim curriculum models are

> .... socially constructed. They are designed by adults with particular beliefs about what constitutes appropriate activities for children at a particular moment in history. The beliefs of these adults emanate from the dominant values of the culture and society [.....] within which they live and work.

(1999:80)

Anning and Edwards believe there is a conflict in emphasis and tone used in official guidance between prioritising cognitive aspects of experience and having a broader, more inclusive focus. The differences in language and tone of the curriculum guidance documentation of England, Scotland, Wales and Northern Ireland have not gone unnoticed. It might be argued that comparisons between these have helped establish some degree of rapprochement between the 'hard-edged' language of goals, skills and achievements (for example, in the1996a 'Desirable Outcomes for Learning') and the reassertion of the value and place of play in later curriculum guidance.

This tension between the two views still exists and is particularly acute when we consider not only curriculum content but also the associated pedagogy. Beliefs about young children's learning, the nature of appropriacy in the curriculum and the models of pedagogy that best match these values are the driving forces behind the learning opportunities, resourcing and support we provide for children in early years settings. For our adult convenience, curriculum models classify the totality of children's experiences into categories and domains, which aid discussion and simplify the processes of planning and assessing learning. While children experience learning as a seamless robe, it is for us a coat of many colours, each to be thought of as a curriculum area.

Organising Curriculum Guidance

In the UK context there is general agreement about the 'colours' of the learning domains that constitute the planned curriculum. All UK countries have identified language development as key although terms vary. Physical development is included in all four, as is Knowledge and Understanding of the World, although in Scotland this also includes Mathematical experiences. Scientific and technological understandings are sometimes explicitly mentioned and at others subsumed in broader definitions. Creative and aesthetic development as well as personal, social and emotional development are also included, sometimes under different headings. All guidance documents acknowledge the place of play in early learning, the importance of adult roles and the need for maintaining close links between the child's world inside and outside the educational setting. While there is considerable emphasis on the quality of provision made available to children and the constructive nature of their learning there is also an element of instruction and even of Papert's 'schoolish kinds of learning'. There is little explicit mention of the place ICT can occupy in supporting learning, although clearly Knowledge and Understanding of the World subsumes an awareness of the place of technologies in everyday life. In examining the place of ICT in the Early Years curriculum the key questions for me relate to:

- using ICT in a developmentally appropriate way
- supporting creative, exploratory and playful applications of ICT in specific curriculum areas
- getting the balance between construction, instruction and adult direction right
- giving careful consideration to the roles of the adults in school and out.

Developmentally appropriate use of ICT in the curriculum

The idea that resources to support learning be subject to scrutiny is not new. Even the newest parents make hundreds of rapid-on-the-spot decisions about what is safe for their baby to have as playthings. They make aesthetic judgements, consider value for money, child attention, value some cultural norms, bear in mind the fitness of the item for the purpose in hand, the ease of availability, the usefulness of others' recommendations and so on. There is nothing intrinsically different about the decisions educators make in schools except that they need to establish clear learning outcomes with children of differing abilities from diverse backgrounds. Experienced practitioners already know about such decision making and can draw upon this knowledge confidently when considering ICT resourcing.

Specific guidance is available from bodies such as the National Association for the Education of Young Children (NAEYC), website: http://www.naeyc.org/ Careful consideration of several issues connected with the use of technology by young children has been linked to research studies in that particular area. The issues concern:

- the teacher's essential role in evaluating appropriate uses of technology
- potential benefits of appropriate use of technology in early childhood programs
- the integration of technology into the typical learning environment
- equitable access to technology, including children with special needs
- stereotyping and violence in software
- the role of teachers and parents as advocates
- the implications of technology for professional development.

I have drawn upon these pages elsewhere (Cook, 2000) to consider appropriate practice, ICT and early literacy.

Software

An important aspect of resource decision making relates to software choices. Making evaluative decisions about software we intend to purchase is directly related to the learning outcomes we have in mind, to developmental appropriacy and to striking the right balance between the tensions already outlined. Software for young children should be easy for them to use but not try to make learning simplistic. Children should be able to find out easily what they can get the program to do rather than have it close all options down so that only one routeway to a predetermined end is possible. Papert seized upon the term used by two kindergarten pupils about work with computers, 'hard fun', as describing well the challenge and engagement that comes with meaningful learning. He (1996) outlines objectionable features of software as:

• *giving agency to the machine and not the child*

By this he means seeing children only as 'answering machines' not recognising the strengths they bring to learning. Very young children need opportunities to explore, to point and click and see what happens. Providing just enough guidance helps build confidence that this is something they can do by themselves. Adults need to give careful thought to the nature and timing of their interventions.

• *being deceptive and proud of it*

What he has in mind here is software that promotes itself by claiming something along the lines that this is such fun your children won't realise they are learning. As adults we need to take care we do not impose on children our perceptions that learning is difficult. Slipping mathematics or anything else subversively into children's learning programs is taking the wrong approach; rather we should find mathematics they love doing and use this as a starting point. Electronic worksheets are still worksheets to practise skills even when presented on screen and seem to have child appeal and motivational power.

• *favouring quick reactions over long term thinking*

This is a criticism, Papert says, often levelled against video games but which is also true of much question and answer software. Just providing immediate feedback of the right/wrong/try again variety is insufficient to promote problem solving, abstraction or conceptualisation. What video games do very well is reward success with an increased level of challenge at certain points. Children enjoy this as much as adults. Good software needs to offer challenge at a variety of levels to complement children's varying needs.

Much good software currently available does not treat the child as an answering machine, allows easy access and experimentation, encourages children to play constructively with a range of ideas, is easily navigated and has bright, colourful and uncluttered screens. Much of the creativity in curriculum applications still comes from teachers' imaginative use of the more open-ended materials available to them and linking these to learning activities in such a way that ICT adds an extra dimension to the learning or even transforms it.

Creative, exploratory and playful applications of ICT

'Play' is a word with a myriad meanings; when we use it in association with learning it has serious implications for practice and for us as practitioners. As adults we still need to play, sometimes with objects and even more often with ideas, especially when we have new learning opportunities to explore. Just as we enjoy and recognise the value of our playing with, and alongside, children in the sand or imaginative play area then so do we need to engage with, and enjoy playing around with the computer. Such play is probably the best opportunity to get to know the resources currently available. Even when it is not possible to include children in such playful explorations personal computer use makes a significant contribution to professional understandings. Listing the different ways you have used ICT in the last week can produce an interesting set of items. I found asking myself about when I last set myself a personal challenge to use the computer to learn something new or that really interested me produced an answer that was revealing and not too comfortable. Not to be able to play and explore strategies and resources makes it more difficult to see all the learning potential within the equipment available. It is also helpful occasionally to be reminded of what it feels like to be a new learner.

Personal, social and emotional development

The negative aspects associated with stereotypical views of computer use have been very pervasive. I emphasise again that it is the developmentally appropriate use of computers, integrated into a broad range of activities used in a social context in a balanced way, that is important whether the child is at home or at school or nursery. The careful evaluation of software and websites is essential as they are not neutral but contain images and messages from which children will learn much about the world. Every one of the inclusivity criteria used when selecting books, pictures and toys is just as relevant here: for example, ensuring even representation of genders and roles, representing different cultural backgrounds, family groupings, ages and abilities and taking care not to promote violence. These resource materials need to promote the positive values we wish to endorse by depicting people or characters acting co-operatively, sharing and valuing friendship and respecting the rights and feelings of others.

Using computers to encourage children to create jointly composed pictures may offer some realistic experiences of co-operation and collaboration. This can be done when children are separated by long distance, using the internet or e-mail to send pictures backwards and forwards or within a school or classroom. Promoting talk about technology, the creative activity and collaboration all make important contributions to the social aspects of the task..

Many early years settings have used still and video photographs as both a record of children's activities and achievements and as the starting point for discussions. As Mavers and Lakin (2001) point out 'going digital' has many advantages. The most obvious is the immediacy of access: images can be brought into action as quickly as required and shown on a computer screen can be discussed collectively. Mavers and Lakin suggest that this activity can contribute substantially to children's self-esteem and their ability to become involved in decision making about significant moments in their learning. Making images available to parents and carers, either electronically or as printouts has, as they point out, considerable value for home-school links and for the creation of electronic portfolios for record keeping. What does seem clear is that harnessing ICT power as this nursery has done allows them to promote communication, collaboration, positive social values and self-esteem in an exciting and dynamic way. Such activities require children and adults to work together but this the authors see as beneficial. The children learn from watching adults, hear the correct technical language and see procedures in a meaningful context as part of everyday activity.

Finding opportunities for parents and carers to play with their child and the computer is important. Creating times when grown-ups can do this helps develop understanding about the contribution ICT makes to the curriculum. The learning potential within the planned activity should be as clear as possible, especially the difference that ICT makes.

Physical development

Staff should be aware of the health and safety aspects of computer use, especially as much available equipment was not designed with small people in mind. It is important that equipment is safely positioned for users. Chairs, desks and screens should be at the correct height and of the right quality and arranged for social chat and for watchers to observe, learn and gain confidence. The activity should not be overused by any child, but this seems unlikely if it is integrated into an exciting, varied and balanced curriculum.

Much fine motor physical co-ordination is required in many ICT activities and at first it may take time for children to realise the 'cause and effect' relationship between their hand actions with fingers, mouse, key board or light pen and the end results. Once this has happened then 'point and click' comes about readily. The best way to acquire the fine motor skills required here is by having time to play, experiment and explore. Children need some help, and will probably frequently close programs down but with carefully chosen software appropriate for beginners they will learn for themselves. Software with clear screens, simple instructions either with verbal support or picture icons and with 'teacher-lockability' in terms of opening or closing programs is most appropriate here. Children use all their senses to learn and multi-media support maximises opportunity.

Mitra and Rana (2001) describe how children in some disadvantaged Indian communities learned how to operate the 'hole-in-the wall' computer that appeared one day without explanation. These children who did not have access to English learned to operate the computer just by playing. In one case the children managed the very successful strategy of getting 'just in time help' by seeking out the one adult in their community who had some computer experience.

Language and literacy development

Kress (1997) reminds us how broadly we should cast our nets when considering the ways in which children learn to be literate. He asks us to consider forms of representation as unexpected as building with bricks, arranging household objects (cushions, rugs and so on), mark making of various kinds including experiments with pictures, print, plans, and diagrams. In becoming literate children need to understand the symbolism in all of these by 'reading', or interpreting them, and 'writing', or creating them. Labbo (1996) suggests that as adults we need to understand the ways in which children react to and interact with symbolic representations and screens. Reinking (1994) points out that a generation accustomed to multi-media and hypertext presentations in everyday life will have many understandings about what it means to be literate, including some that are different from those of their teachers. The path to literacy of each generation will be different from that of their predecessors. Remembering Papert's advice not to use new learning tools to help us teach as we were taught is consequently very important. Defining what it means to be literate is complex and literacy boundaries evolve rapidly. We need to offer children as many ways of making meaning with symbols as we can and not confine learning with ICT to 'drill and practice'.

Computers, when correctly located and used should foster talk and interaction between adults and children and between children and their peers and siblings when playing and experimenting together. Even 'watchers' learn about talk and should be allowed to participate quietly in this way as long as they wish. The role of adults in fostering talk about computer activities, and in 'on-screen' and 'off-screen' interactions, can challenge children's thinking as well as help them understand how to use the resources.

A wide range of child-friendly software is available to support appropriate literacy work, from open-ended packages with multiple applications (e.g. Kidpix and Kidpixstudio) to specifically designed paint and word processing programs. Such software gives control to children by allowing open-ended, playful explorations and experiments. Pictures can be drawn, marks of all kinds made which replicate pencils, pens and giant markers. Children can experiment with the keyboard, have fun exploring punctuation marks and other symbols, use stamps, make 'repeats' and change the colour, size and style of their creations. More recent programs allow different parts of children's work to be easily moved from one application or another.

A study by Shrader (1990) found that children's computer writing development mirrors closely that made with conventional tools. Children choose to use computers as readily as crayons, pencils and markers as well as to create signs and stories, send messages, and make notes and lists. Clay's concepts about print (1975) were used to compare the mark-making processes and creations. When children's experiments with print are supported by sounds, as with talking word processors, then the possibilities increase. Moving children onto more conventional orthography can be accomplished gradually when appropriate. This helps them develop in both the transcription and compositional elements of writing. Finding their way around the keyboard or having the control to 'write' with the 'draw' tools, knowing which are pictures and which text, having confidence that they can do it, all seem good foundations to build on for the more instructional phase.

Electronic 'talking books' are not intended as substitutes for all the experiences that come from a rich and loving sharing of a favourite story, but they do offer different, but equally valuable, forms of joint interaction with a trusted and loved adult. These complementary experiences offer a great deal of support for more independent engagements with texts. As with any other book experience choosing good material is the secret. If a text would not be accepted if it were a print item then it most certainly will not be worth having electronically. What is important is the quality of the text, illustrations and reading support as well as the operational simplicity. As practitioners we need to be clear about the pedagogical strategy and learning outcomes we intend to implement for those children who have moved beyond introductory explorations.

Creative and aesthetic development

ICT use offers children another tool to use in exploring ideas and creating representations. Where images of different kinds can be integrated with sounds and music then ICT transforms what children can achieve and allows them to create something not possible in any other way. Making images and music electronically offers a novel approach to learning that still allows children to create and evaluate their own products. Electronic paint doesn't work like everyday paint, the colours behave differently, images can be repeated, enlarged, multiplied and reversed or even linked to particular sounds. ICT makes it possible for children to explore and experiment with line, shape, colour and pattern. Creative activity can make a rich contribution to learning in other curriculum areas as well as the aesthetic domain and electronic explorations should sit alongside work with other media and be one technique among many others.

Making music, listening and responding to it centres primarily around expressing feelings and emotions. Technology of all kinds has in recent years increased the range of musical experiences available to children and changes the ways in which they can interact with it. Again ICT extends the range of techniques and musical ideas (the sounds of different instruments, rhythm, pitch, volume, mood) that children can play around with in ways not possible without this support. Resources on CD-ROM or the Internet allow teachers and children to extend their repertoire of songs and traditional rhymes for enjoyment and as a support for literacy activities.

Using ICT in imaginative role-play situations offers support to many areas of learning. It helps children develop their **Knowledge and understanding of the world**, contributes to their social and personal learning and to their cognitive development in both literacy and mathematics. One nursery I know uses a set of small robust notepads in thematic play activities such as 'the estate agents' as just another resource. Notepads are about the size of an A4 sheet of paper, light, portable and relatively inexpensive, have easily rechargeable batteries and are compatible with other computers and printers. In this nursery one is also available on the writing table as another tool alongside pencils, pens and markers, paper clips, scissors and related thematic materials. Staff introduce the notepads to children by playing with them as well as finding opportunities to discuss letters, words or numbers. Learning 'about' events as well as having opportunities to re-enact them are the learning objectives: there is no expectation that children will create a printed product. Though any child who wishes to go further with the notepad is encouraged to do so. Children's computer writing is included in the nursery produced books, which in turn become a further reading resource. The notepads can go home to support home-school projects also. As these machines have conventional keyboards then this exploratory play helps children begin to sort out alphabetic symbols from numerical ones. Since many children are bilingual then this type of use facilitates staff/parent dialogue about the similarities and differences amongst the many community languages.

One reception class teacher involved in an ICT project about effective teaching noted her dissatisfaction with much of the software available at the time to support the early **mathematics** work she felt some of her children needed. She wanted to create meaningful and varied opportunities for children to practise aspects of counting. The report of her work (Mosley, *et al.*, 1999) makes fascinating reading. She describes how she used the stamping facility of certain software to help children create 'counting pictures', which then became incorporated into a wide range of classroom activities. In creating and sharing these pictures the children counted and recounted things many times because it was an important part of the process. They also created 'counting houses' which moved them on to the ideas of grouping numbers and sets of the same kind of object. Counting songs were also re-created. Once the children were familiar with operating the program they continued the creative work without adult support. The teacher was able to concentrate on the teaching and learning elements as and when she thought necessary.

Mathematics is not only about helping children understand numbers and counting but also about developing confidence and enthusiasm in using mathematical knowledge in a range of situations. Most early years settings find creative ways of using roamers, pixies and other programmable toys. 'Customised' versions of roamer or Pip are directed by children to make visits around the group at circle time, or play a part in story re-enactments by carrying out the command sequences that will take them to each of the three little pigs' houses in turn.

Exploring the world scientifically through CD-ROMs or the Internet opens up perspectives that go beyond pictures and text and allow children to begin to understand what the world is like for other people. Complementary to the range of lenses, magnifiers and other viewers are computer microscopes. They are worth borrowing from other classes, even if only for a few hours. Because the magnified images are displayed on screen they are big, bright and easily seen by small (and bigger) people who have difficulty closing one eye and looking at the same time. These are really intended for older children and have many additional features but watching a caterpillar munch is magic and not just to be kept for big kids!

Achieving and maintaining balance: construction, instruction and initiation

Acknowledging that computers can be as well or as badly used as any other resource, Papert, and others, are concerned that the power of computers may be used with the teaching strategies of a former period. That is to support adult directed activity. Inappropriately used ICT does not contribute much to learning: for example, when computers are used to keep children busy, as a reward or motivating tool or simply to practise skills. Young children should enjoy playful and exploratory ICT use in support of learning but not experience too much instruction too soon. We as adults are aware of our duty to help children understand the world and consequently there is a tension between supporting 'construction' and giving 'instruction'. There is a place for both; the critical factor is getting the balance right by establishing clearly focussed learning outcomes for both adult and child initiated activity. There is little to be gained if learners are frustrated by not knowing what they need to know when they need to know it. Also, those working in school settings frequently assert how impossible it is to wait for the spontaneous emergence of just the right moment for each child to occur. As children reach the end of the Foundation stage, there is a requirement to ensure that they become familiarised with the formal demands of the teaching approaches they will experience at the next stage; instruction will be one of these. Professional judgements are not always easy to make, but to see computers as merely useful in an 'instructional' sense would be to seriously underestimate the potential of ICT as a means of transforming learning.

Roles of Adults

The importance of adults and children sharing interactions has percolated through much of this text, and supporting learning has been seen as a two-way process in every curriculum area. Adults have a significant role in providing and resourcing learning environments, guiding children's interaction with the experiences offered, granting sufficient challenge to learners and carefully observing the outcome of how and with whom the children choose to learn. Such observations provide the basis for ongoing planning and assessment. We have learned much in recent years from research about the amount of early literacy and mathematical learning that takes place informally and incidentally. These studies have shown how frequently this learning goes unrecognised in educational contexts: this would seem to be equally true of computer use. Research, mostly with older pupils, suggests that computer use at school lags behind that in the home in quantity, quality and variety. It would be odd if this did not also affect the lives of younger children especially those with older siblings. Papert sees this mismatch as one of the key driving forces for rethinking educational practices. Liaison between parents, carers and practitioners is essential to ensure that early learning is used as an effective foundation. Where these home opportunities have not been available we must ensure that provision in the early years setting offers equity of experience. This may mean a directive role for the adults as such children may be reluctant to engage in ICT related activities. Adult intervention, direction and encouragement to participate are critical if we are to avoid further distance between the digital 'haves' and 'have-nots'. We need to share what we know about ICT and learning with children's parents as they know a great deal more about their own children than we will ever learn but also they might be well placed to use our insights constructively in their homes.

Adults have several important roles in facilitating and enhancing learning with computers. Perhaps one of the most important is knowing when to intervene and when to stand back and let children take the initiative. While children will, as the Mitra and Rana study shows, find out a great deal for themselves adult help is useful when needed. Supportive adults are one help-line for children. They understand how programs operate, can model overlooked functions, extend children's thinking by questions and prompts and discovering 'teachable moments'. They can encourage co-operation and collaboration between children and ensure the integration of computer activities into the overall curriculum. They can be 'troubleshooters' when, as is inevitable, problems arise not just with the hardware and software but with 'mouse wars' and 'arcade game clicking' (see Labbo et al., 2000). Finally adults can introduce more formalised approaches to learning when appropriate. There is a valid place for practising acquired skills, gaining speed and fluency with counting, computation and orthographic conventions as well as building computer competence. But let us also exploit the playful potential of ICT when this is the most developmentally appropriate means of access to learning for the children we have in our care.

Conclusion

Great claims have been made about technology and learning by both advocates and detractors. Claims about change and the future are risky at any time and in an area of such rapid advances are asking to be proved wrong. Papert talks about the gap between 'someday and Monday' that we teachers sometimes experience, that is we believe that teaching and learning will be changed in unimaginable ways by this type of technology but in the meantime there is a need to teach in the situation we find ourselves in. His response is that to have a vision of what we would like to do will guide us towards the 'someday'. To help children maximise their learning, educators need the facilities to help them achieve this end. We may need to use our collective professional voice to argue our case strongly in a number of arenas for the best equipment and the most appropriate pedagogy for us to use with our young learners. After all, trying to keep up with our wonderful biological computers is the best and most exciting 'hard fun'.

References

Anning, A. and Edwards, A. (1999) *Promoting Children's Learning from Birth to Five*, Open University Press, Buckingham, England

Cook, D. (2001) Meeting the challenge: ICT, Early literacy and the role of the Educator, *Education* 3-13, Vol. 29, no1, March

Cook, D. and Finlayson, H. (1999) *Interactive Children, Communicative Teaching*, OU Press, Buckingham England

Gopnik, A., Meltzoff, A. and Kuhl, P. (1999) *How babies think*, Weidenfield and Nicolson, London, UK

Kress, G. (1997) *Before Writing: Re-thinking the Path to literacy*, Routledge, London

Haughland, S. (1997) *Selecting Developmentally Appropriate Software*, available at http://www.childrenandcomputers.com/Articles/selecting_developmentally_approp, htm

Labbo, L. D. (1996) A semiotic analysis of young children's symbol making in a classroom computer centre, reading *Research Quarterly*, 31 (1) 356-383

Labbo, L. D., Sprague, l., Montero, M,K. and Font, G. (2000) Connecting a computer centre to themes, literature and kindergarteners' literacy needs, *Reading Online* 4(1) July 2000, available at http://www.reading online.org/electronic/labbo/

National Association for the Education of Young Children (1996) *Technology and Young children*, available from pubaff@naeyc.org, updated Feb. 1998

Marsh, J. and Thompson, P. (2001) *Parental involvement in literacy development: using media texts*, paper presented to British Educational Research Association conference, Leeds 2001

Mavers, D. and Lakin, I. (2001) Look what I did today, in *Beyond the School Gates*, Newman College with MAPE, Castlefield Publishers, Northampton , UK

Mitra, S.and Rana, V. (2001) Children and the Internet: experiments with minimally invasive education in India, *British Journal of Educational Technology*, vol. 32, No 2, pp.221-232

Mosley, D., Higgins,S., Bramald, R., Hardman, F., Miller, J., Mroz, M., Tse, H., Newton, D., Thompson, I., Williamson, J., Halligan, J., Bramald. S., Newton, L., Tymms, P., Henderson, B. and Stout, J. (1999) *Ways Forward with ICT: Effective pedagogy using ICT for literacy and numeracy in Primary Schools*, University of Newcastle, UK

Papert, S. (1996) *The connected family; Bridging the digital generation gap*, Longstreet Press Atlanta, Georgia USA

Reinking, D. (1994) Electronic Literacy, *(Perspectives in Reading Research*, No 4), Athens, University of Georgia, National Reading Research Center

Shrader (1990) The word processor as a tool for young writers, in Yost, N. (circa 1999) *Emerging Literacy: crayons, markers, pencils and computer experiences*, available at http://childrenandcomputers.com/Articles/emerging_literacy.htm

SPA Consumer Market Report, 1996

ICT Capability and Initial Teacher Training

Babs Dore and Cathy Wickens

This chapter tracks the development of ideas and practice in response to the requirement that Initial Teacher Training students develop confidence and competence in their use of ICT both to support their own developing professional need and to be able to teach effectively with ICT in the classroom. We discuss the evolution of our thinking over a three-year cycle of teaching and reflection. During this time we recognised that, in solving the specific challenge, we had produced materials that could usefully be offered to a much wider range of students as a self-supported online resource. We highlight also the impact of changing government requirements for Initial Teacher Training and university initiatives to wider student access to online support for learning.

The demands of embedding ICT capability into Initial Teacher Training have caused many institutions, including our own, to critically consider the ways in which provision can support this. For institutions within the UK the constraints of Annex B of 4/98 (*High Status, High Standards*), the National Curriculum for Initial Teacher Training, required student teachers to be able to assimilate ICT into their subject teaching with a high degree of competence and understanding. Although many students now start their Initial Teacher Training as users of word processing, e-mail and Internet, many still lack a level of competence and confidence in the use of ICT. This is a problem that industry addresses daily with their workforce, but education is concerned not with the skills one has but with the judgements of what one can do with whatever skills one possesses. Therefore this chapter will make reference to Annex B of 4/98 but the issues are pertinent to all those involved in Initial Teacher Training.

> Technology applied to the development of a 'humanistic, democratic, learner centred environment, controlled and directed by students and teachers' stands in contrast to the rhetoric of targets, training, investment returns and accountability mechanisms which pervades so many central government communications to the educational system.
>
> (Muffoletto 1996)

Wild (1995) identifies a range of factors that affect uptake of ICT by students and new teachers including confidence, attitude, expertise and organisation. He suggests that it is important that students are able to identify a purpose for ICT early in their course and are able to reflect on ICT use for learning and teaching. The module content should then relate forward to the continuing experience of the student with ICT both in the taught and the school experience element of their course. A growing understanding of the nature of ICT and its contribution to learning and how children interact with ICT should then become an integral part of their teaching.

> It may not always be easy for students to transfer their personal skills in IT to using them in the classroom, and if they are to do so they may need opportunity, facilities and considerable encouragement and support from their training establishments and schools.
>
> Cuckle, P., Clarke, S. & Jenkins, I. (2000:10)

This chapter records the development of a module which aimed to meet these needs, in particular in auditing their ICT capability, but within a framework that would enthuse the students and develop capability rather than skills.

> IT capability is characterised by an ability to use effectively IT tools and information sources to analyse, process and present information, and to model, measure and control external events.
>
> Poole P. (1998:10)

Their experiences in this module formed a starting point from which they began to develop their own competence in the use of ICT. This initially met their needs as student teachers but would also subsequently influence their consideration of the place of ICT within the primary curriculum. In acknowledging this we felt it was important to employ a range of techniques in our own teaching in an attempt to introduce the students to a developing pedagogy for the use of ICT in education. This resulted in a move away from an initial 'training' model of delivery to a much more interactive approach with practical activities firmly rooted in context and designed to encourage exploration and collaboration in building understanding.

Skills training?

Whilst students starting initial teacher training have been accepted on academic merit, they bring to the course a wide range of competence and confidence in their study skills. Therefore as with most higher education institutions an attempt is made during the induction period to provide a baseline in support of these needs, and part of this package includes ICT 'skills training'. Guest, G & Hughes, M. (1999) disagree with this principle arguing that discrete elements of ICT courses should concentrate on pedagogy and classroom applications rather than ICT skills, and that students wanting ICT skills should have these taught in the context of classroom applications. However the individual needs of the students was considerable, ranging from those who had successfully taken 'A' level Information Technology to those who were terrified to switch the machine on.

> Not that confident but have used computers more now that I've come to University. I'm not scared of using them though I also think I will break it when I'm using it

Anxiety, lack of confidence, want to improve desperately
(Student Teachers' comments during the optional study skills module)

Our 'skills training' module was optional and had a simple objective that students should be able to use ICT confidently to research and submit their first assignments. However, we presumed that the students would make an informed choice! The distractions of a new environment whatever the background of the student can mean that 'optional' can be interpreted as just that and the implications for their future learning are not understood. Possibly naively, this was accepted as the baseline of competence for the audit module that was to take place in the second semester of year 1, the cohort coming from a four-year BA Hons Primary Education with QTS course.

Development of ideas

The content and context of the module highlights issues that trouble education professionals. If the assessable outcome is to adhere to external criteria be it for GCSE, National Curriculum Programmes of Study or the requirements of 4/98, then should this be the starting point for the thought process or should there be higher ideals and aspirations? It was certainly hard not to feel the whip of the criteria but one of our overriding objectives was that students should have a positive learning experience and although this module was not about the use of ICT in school, our own practice should demonstrate a pedagogy of ICT that they could emulate when on school placement.

In order for student teachers … to integrate the technology skills needed, they first need to be taught by those who value such experiences and who use these skills in their professional practice.

Fisher, M. (2000:112)

We concluded that we could justify our decision as this was to be a pass/fail module and part of the criteria for assessment included working on their own learning plan. Mapping against the criteria was rightly done as one of the final activities and we were pleasantly surprised that whilst we never expected to cover all of the criteria adequately in such a short space of time, we had covered more than we first envisaged. We recognised that we need not be constrained by the demands of an imposed curriculum but could use this opportunity to begin to address the development of more transferable skills when learning about ICT.

The drill and practice, out of context approach adopted in the optional skills module was, we knew, a poor model of learning if we wished to move to a more self-supported student approach. Consequently it was important to identify the goals for learning in the subsequent audit module as not being simply the acquisition of skills in response to the demands of 4/98 but that students should begin to develop:
a) an understanding of the common practices and methods used to produce outcomes across a range of software applications;
b) a recognition that the features of the machine itself, for instance provisionality, support this process;

c) strategies for approaching new tasks and software that depend on a deep understanding of how the computer manages and performs operations and an ability to transfer understanding, knowledge and skills from one application to another;
d) an ability to recognise where use of the computer will aid or enhance completion of a task or activity;
e) a recognition of the range of possibilities that the use of ICT affords.

David Jaques (2000) confronts these issues, citing Kolb (1984) who makes three assumptions that we felt echoed our own rationale:

1. We learn best when we are personally involved in the learning experience.
2. Knowledge of any kind has more significance when we learn it through our own initiative, insight and discovery.
3. Learning is best when we are committed to aims that we have been involved in setting, when our participation with others is valued and when there is a supporting framework in which to learn.

Kolb in Jaques (2000:vii)

These assumptions informed our initial planning. By making explicit our learning outcomes, and how we saw the module content and delivery supporting these, we involved the students in auditing their own capability and identifying their own needs. Student commitment to the aims of the module would further be fostered by encouraging participation in a group task which was designed to be challenging yet enjoyable.

This was a short module of twelve hours contact time spread over six weeks, with groups in excess of twenty-five, timetabled in a room containing approximately eighteen computers. Access to peripherals such as digital cameras was limited. We realised that much work would have to be done in pairs and that non-contact tasks would not have to rely solely on access to equipment. What appeared to be a problem was in fact at the heart of how we envisaged the learning taking place. Vygotsky (in Lachs, V. 2000:26) celebrates this pedagogy as a 'fertile ground for learning' discussing the ZPD (zone of proximal development) where learning takes place in the gap between what students can do on their own and what they can do with help of an adult or more capable peer. Thus learning happens within a social context, mediated by language, and becomes culture specific. Those who are more capable aid the process by acting as a 'scaffolders' of learning.

Collaboration produces a joint product created from a shared understanding where the group is an arena for discussion and development. The collaboration between group members will allow people to hear other people's views, build on each other's ideas, and make joint decisions and develop and learn in the process.

Vygotsky (in Lachs, V. 2000:27)

The nature and size of groups when the result is to be an individual piece of work is one that dogs many teachers especially when the use of IT can mask the outcome. It was decided after some debate about issues such as plagiarism, effort and hiding behind a partner's expertise, that given their maturity students should self-select their groups, pairs were preferable and we would monitor use or abuse of the technology.

We wanted to move away from a model that supported transmission of knowledge about common applications to a more active, collaborative mode emphasising learning in context. Our vehicle for supporting this was to be the use of a multimedia-authoring package. Experience in previous years of introducing students to multimedia authoring suggested that the demands of such software encouraged students to develop a deeper understanding of how the computer (and our network) functions. We concluded that here was a way of encouraging students to take control of their own learning, within a tutor-supported environment. The essential interactivity of multimedia authoring would encourage students to reflect on their actions and articulate their developing understanding of the features of the package itself.

> They will come up against problems such as wanting to make the program do something that is beyond their abilities, which they will need to solve by using imagination and compromise. ..... how to design multimedia as an integrated whole, how to create the non-linear environment and how to make the piece interactive and usable by the audience.
>
> Lachs, V (2000:7)

The demands of the task meant that students would need to acquire and store a range of different media (text, sound, audio and video) effectively and then manipulate these in a number of applications so that they could be accessed by the authoring software. Being an effective and innovative user of ICT requires the building of a mental model of how the computer handles input and performs common functions. Students needed to appreciate that simple functions and procedures are common to many applications and can result in similar outcomes. Our students would need to develop a level of understanding of how the computer facilitated such actions in order to produce a working presentation.

> We need to focus on educating and supporting the appropriate applications of technology rather than on the tool itself. Individual expertise, prior knowledge of curriculum, teacher needs and learning styles need to be explicitly incorporated into the knowledge transfer process with the creation of new knowledge as a result.
>
> Fisher, M. (2000:111)

We knew from our own experience that when multimedia authoring, gathering resources such as sound, video and graphics can be enormously time consuming. This is an integral part of the process and to miss out any of its constituent parts would negate the outcomes.

> ..like an authoring shell. It offers a framework for drawing together the (different) media into an interactive environment, but the different media would have to be created

separately in painting programs, animation programs, sound files and word processors and then imported into the authoring program.

Lachs, V. (2000:174)

Early on in the planning stage we decided that the context would be themselves as new students at the university. This meant we could confidently include in the task use of digital stills and video, sound and scanning as all this was available either in the workshop or on campus.

Putting it all together in the classroom.

After such extensive planning we began the first session with a degree of optimism that we would be compensated for all our time and effort with a smoothly running module. In many respects this was the outcome but there were also issues that came to light, which we hadn't anticipated and eventually necessitated a change of approach. In order to track and assess the success of our planning we asked the students to complete entry and exit expectations and evaluation questionnaires. About half the students completed both. We have already hinted that our baseline presumption was incorrect in that, if appropriate, they would all attend the optional study skills sessions. The reality was that a significant number successfully found ways of masking their lack of capability or had misjudged their own ability in relation to the stated outcomes of the ICT study skills sessions. Some students over-estimated their own capability, and such comments as, 'I can do it on my computer at home' were not uncommon.

> ... the reality that all teachers surely recognise – that students do not transfer their knowledge across different settings, that there is a problem relating theory to practice i.e. that knowledge seems to be context-related. Perhaps some ideal final product could be represented as a knowledge structure, but learning is more realistically seen as an activity and knowledge as an aspect of that activity, and therefore not easily abstracted from it.
>
> Laurillard, D. (1993:15)

Overview of the module content and issues covered

1. **Introduction and Overview**
    Annex B of the Curriculum for Initial Teacher Training
    ICT Survey
    The ICT Audit document and portfolio of evidence
    Introduction to the school of education IT facilities - Firewall
    Accessing applications
    File management
    Internet quiz (*this was a fun activity requiring simple searching, then copying and pasting answers into a word processed table*)

2. **Using the Internet**
   Use of the University of Brighton Intranet (Silver)
   Practical issues in using the Internet
   The Internet for professional use
   Evaluating the quality of information found on Internet
   Using Internet to find information, presenting the information in a spreadsheet
   (*Again a fun activity where students were asked to price a desktop computer system to a budget, looking for information on the Internet and other sources and using a spreadsheet to calculate and present their findings*)

3. **Introduction to Multimedia (Mediator)**
   Why learn how to author multimedia?
   Multimedia authoring – basic techniques
   Planning for Multimedia project – sessions 4 and 5
   Tutorial – how to use Mediator
   Graphics, sound and video – inputting and downloading
   Use of scanner and digital camera

4. **Developing competence in ICT – experience rooted in context**
   Working in pairs produce the 'electronic' guide to being a student using a variety of resources, scanned images, digital camera pictures, items downloaded from Internet etc.

5. **Presentation of multimedia work**
   Using ICT for professional purposes

6. **Review**
   Where now?
   Completion of Audit, development of realistic action plan
   Building an ICT portfolio – what is evidence?

As can be seen from the outline of sessions, the emphasis in the module was on gaining 'experiential knowledge' and about learning precepts within an enjoyable fun environment. The first three sessions were designed to give students the knowledge, skills and understanding to undertake the paired activity in sessions four and five and to complete their audit and action plan in session six.

When surveyed at the first session, many students felt themselves confident with basic applications (word processing assignments) and were keen to learn more but 30% expressed feelings of uncertainty, inadequacy or frustration in their use.

> '*Tragic! I get confused and frustrated on the internet.*'
> '*I don't use it to the best of my ability! I do the bare minimum!*'
> '*I would like to be a lot more confident as I feel I lack understanding of important aspects.*'
> '*Need to develop skills and confidence ...*'

'I am willing to learn but I would rather avoid them. I'm not confident at all.'
'Apprehensive, worried about whether I will be competent enough.'
'Afraid of them – I don't know how they really work.'
' ... time consuming with limited experience ...'

Expectations centred on broadening knowledge of different ICT applications, the development of ICT skills and effective use of the Internet with a heavy emphasis, even from those who had not expressed concern, with building up confidence.

Progress for the anxious was tentative and patchy until halfway through session three when the students were encouraged to explore and have fun with multimedia, working in pairs for support. Increasingly ripples of delight were heard around the room as a link was successful, stifled giggles as sounds were added randomly and a general rise in conversation as groups began to share their success and learn from each other. Much of the practical teaching to this point had been through a series of fairly prescriptive structured tasks giving little opportunity for variety of outcome. The introduction to multimedia however had been specifically taught using scaffolding as an approach.

> If students are learning through a constructivist model then once they have grasped basic skills they need to feel ownership of the skills. They then begin a mastery of skills in a more global context and finally are able to use multiple perspectives in problem solving.
>
> Guest, G. & Hughes, M. (1999)

Laurillard (1993) extends the discussion of social constructivism from Vygotsky's description of children's learning to learning in Higher Education.

> ... (teaching) must emulate the success of everyday learning by contextualising, situating knowledge in real-world activity.
>
> Laurillard (1993:29)

Judging by their response it appeared that to foster this increasing autonomy we were correct to lead them gently and then allow them to trial new competencies within a safe environment. As one student reported:

> ' ... an opportunity to try out many newly acquired skills and practice old ones.'

Sessions four and five demonstrated this effectively as they supported each other, learned at their own pace and made us almost redundant at times! Many of the questions we were asked involved technical issues easily fielded by a learning technologist or technician rather than teaching staff. We questioned how much contact we needed with them early in the module in session two, which was taught from an interactive worksheet on the network share folder. Our expensive but underused skills module in the first semester plus our questions over face-to-face delivery in the early part of the audit module in the second semester were ones we needed to address at the evaluation stage.

The assessment task was to compile a portfolio of evidence from the activities and complete and action plan their initial audit. Although a presentation of the multimedia task was part of the activities it wasn't part of the assessment criteria. We questioned the rigour of this decision but decided that it is difficult to assess group work fairly.

> It is very difficult to compare one student with another when the report is the result of a group effort. Students differ in their skills, their rates and levels of working, and their styles of learning. Who is to say that the student who held them together and constantly inspired the group yet contributed nothing to the report should receive no academic reward?
>
> Jaques D. (2000:148)

Attendance at all of the sessions was not compulsory as long as usual university procedures for absence had been adhered to and an assessment portfolio submitted. For the majority of the students their enthusiasm for the task, commitment to their studies and a sense of fair play to their partner meant that the quality of the presentations was good and the portfolio and action plan thorough and thoughtful. Some students commented in the exit questionnaire that they would have liked the presentation to have counted towards the assessment. More worryingly we monitored the attendance and were under the distinct impression that some students took advantage of the fact that presentation of the multimedia task was not part of the completion criteria. Therefore, a number of students had missed the opportunity to experience the aims of the module fully. Our initial reservations over working in groups and use of IT masking the quality of the outcome had been substantiated.

The exit questionnaire clearly demonstrated that the content and delivery of the module was keenly appreciated. We asked the students to indicate how they thought their level of confidence in their personal use of ICT had changed during the module. This they indicated on a 1 (low) to 5 (high) scale. Over half (60%) saw themselves moving one point up the scale (2-3, 3-4 or 4-5), whilst of the remaining students 30% felt they had moved on 2 points and about 10% saw no change. They were asked to comment generally on how they saw this module contributing to their developing capability with ICT. Some of those reporting a 2 point movement in confidence wrote:

> *'I now find the computer fun and am not afraid of it anymore.'*
> *'I can even use my own computer without panicking.'*
> *'Yes, less afraid of the whole thing – but I've got a lot to learn. I intend to use my personal computer over the summer to really try to get a grip on the internet etc.'*
> *'I feel I can explore now without the worry of the computer blowing up.'*

The students were then asked to respond specifically on how they thought learning to author multimedia had contributed to the development of their own capability. All replied positively and there were a number of comments that we felt added weight to our own response to the task.

'.. have confidence, know I can make the computer do what I want.'
' just to basically navigate yourself round the system, with my work saving and moving folders'
'brilliant program making all sorts of new things interesting to try on computers ...'
'I felt good when I had achieved it and confident to help others ...'
'It has made me less afraid to try things – it's the only way to learn really.'
'I now feel I would be capable and confident in using any program.'
'Moving between 2 files or programs a lot has built my confidence.'
' ... more confidence to experiment... '
'built confidence in general use.'
'pulls together many facets/skills in a worthwhile way.'
'it gave me more confidence in using ICT and more practice in trouble shooting.'
'it has made me realise how simple and logical ICT is!'
'opened a new door to the use of ICT which I will master!'

Specifically we asked the students how well they thought the multimedia activity had catered for different levels of ability and experience.

'People were able to get on at their own pace for sessions 3,4 and 5.'
'Each student at different levels has achieved a lot.'
'More time was spent on those who needed more help.'

One of the key features of the first year of the module was that students benefited from working in small groups and many acknowledged this in their evaluations.

'The more able students helped the less able with the tasks.'
'... help from other students – teamwork! ...'
'... we helped each other with things we didn't understand.'

Above all, they had fun whilst they learned. It was vital that we didn't lose any of these qualities.

'I can reinforce the knowledge I have learnt by 'playing' in the various applications and now be confident to teach myself new skills'

Face-to-face to online?
When evaluating the module at the semester end the issues seemed straightforward:
• the optional skills module needed revising;
• we needed to reconsider our contact time with the students;
• the presentation should become part of the assessment criteria;
• we needed to address grouping and equity in outcome.

Plus we hoped to think more about:
- how the module would support students' use of ICT elsewhere in the course;
- how the use of multimedia developed their ICT capability.

Colleagues from many subjects and phases had expressed an interest in our approach with multimedia as well as voicing concerns in general about the challenge of implementing and auditing section B of Annex B. Our colleagues teaching in a packed one-year postgraduate setting were asking for a kick-start for their own students' ICT capability so that course tutors could then meaningfully address embedding its use into their subject and teaching practices. In response to their needs, but as an interim measure, we quickly reworked our materials into a series of units that followed much the same content as our original module. These were placed on the University Intranet and also made available via a virtual learning environment (WebCT). The units were all word processed but made some use of interactivity through hyperlinks to relevant web sites, depending on the activity. Some links, such as those to the university on-line tutorials were to support the development of understanding of common applications, word processing, spreadsheets or presentation software for example. Others, such as BECTA, were set within text which prompted the user to reflect on the use of ICT within their own phase or subject specialism. The tasks within each unit followed a similar pattern as our practical and non-contact tasks, such as reading, researching and various fairly prescriptive activities on the computer. These then, as with our original module, led into the main authoring task. Here we used Microsoft PowerPoint as the vehicle, which is more widely available than our original multimedia authoring package. The context was left open although the suggestion was that students should produce a resource that could be used with children during school placement. Wild (1995) advocates this approach, as does Fisher, M. (2000) who investigates the constant challenge for ICT courses in teacher education.

> ...it is suggested that the content of individual courses is developed in line with the need to emphasise the methodology of classroom use of ICT: that is, providing experiences for students to learn how to use computers in their teaching, rather than how to use computers or related technology
>
> Wild (1995:17)

> ...need to focus on supporting beginning computer users with achieving a base comfort level in technology functions, in addition to making the connection between curriculum and instructional strategies.
>
> Fisher, M. (2000:118)

Fisher goes on to discuss approaches to learning that confirm our own findings that skills courses do little to develop capability and that we should be moving towards a pedagogy-based training which is technology rich.

> ...moving away from using introductory technology courses with lots of skill development focusing on 'use for operation' and some integration in curricula, to multiple

infused experiences 'using the tools for application' for technology in teaching, learning and assessment

Fisher, M. (2000:119)

We called this series of units 'Kick-Start, an optional module'. They required no tutor contact at all so we realised that we had turned our original 100% tutor contact to 0% . Where 'Kick-Start' was accessed from the virtual learning environment tutor/student or student/student contact could occur through an asynchronous discussion forum, separated into private areas, organised by subject and phase. These fora proved immediately popular for some groups, numbers involved were small (below 20) and each forum had its own tutor to moderate discussion. However those students who were making best use of 'Kick-Start' were PGCE students who were possibly more used to independent learning. We were also painfully conscious of the lack of sophistication and interactivity in what we were offering online.

The success of our online version and reflection on the progress of the original module prompted us to explore the possibility of reducing our face-to-face contact in place of online learning. However, with large numbers in our module (175 in a year group) we could not reasonably support our students through a discussion forum. We knew we wanted to enable students to become autonomous users of ICT within a supportive environment, but we also wanted to give them flexibility in when and where they learnt and the pace at which they learnt. This we felt could apply equally well to our undergraduate students. Certainly there had been some feedback from the original module suggesting that we needed to acknowledge that some more competent students were keen to work at their own pace, independent of our support.

> *'The beginning of the module did not cater for different needs (Internet and spreadsheet) as some people had no experience. Multimedia did, as you could make your presentation as complicated or as simple as you like.'*

Initiatives within the School of Education had led to the development of a secure Intranet. As a result, 'Kick-Start', having enjoyed only a brief exposure in word-processed format, could now be extensively reworked and web authored. Animated 'Flash' tutorials would replace the original ICT study skills session for undergraduates and offer support to any PGCE students who might benefit. Interactive units such as our introduction to the Internet for professional purposes (session two) would remain in a similar format, as these had been highly successful. Those students without their own computers could access materials more easily on campus through the recently opened Learning Resource Centre. This would give us the opportunity to think about the place of both the study skills and our audit module within this new environment.

Change and development

Within both Initial Teacher Education and ICT things rarely remain static and revision of the requirements for initial teacher training (DfES 2002) meant that our web-authored materials needed early revision to meet the new standards. Also at this point the University began a phased implementation of a Virtual Learning Environment (VLE) in support of student learning so the Kick-Start resource is now easily available to all students registered on initial teacher training or continuing professional development courses. Revision of the BA Primary course in response to changing requirements for training has seen the year one module disappear. It has been replaced by an ICT curriculum module that will address the development of individual ICT capability alongside an introduction to the role of ICT in the primary curriculum. We still acknowledge the importance of addressing students' developing capability early in the course and the Kick-Start materials will form an integral part of the new provision.

The introduction of the VLE across the university has prompted debate on the pedagogical implications of teaching online. The process of development of what eventually became Kick-Start has proved useful as we explore the impact of this on our own teaching. As we developed and refined the materials we attempted to demonstrate good practice in the appropriate use of a range of ICT in delivery. Our experiences have enabled us to initiate a discussion amongst colleagues about the effective use of such technologies within all our courses. Introduction of the VLE and the ability to support student learning through the use of computer mediated communication has encouraged us to consider how we can widen student access to course materials. What elements of our courses would benefit from the students being able to access them when and where they wanted? What are the specific aspects of our course that need to be delivered face-to-face? Equally are there some elements that could be made available online, giving the students more time to interact with them, responding perhaps online or through traditional seminars? How can we give students access to good quality learning materials independent of our taught sessions so that we can concentrate more on reflection, the articulation of practice and sharing of experience?

Brockbank, A. and McGill, I. (1998:5) acknowledge that to become a critical learner, students need not only to be able to reflect upon their own learning but also the learning of others and this has direct implications for the development of the teaching materials.

> For the teacher, the focus moves away from the transmission of the material to how the learners are working with the material in the here and now.
>
> Brockbank, A. and McGill, I. (1998:5)

References

Brockbank, A. and McGill, I. (1998) *Facilitating Reflective Learning in Higher Education* Buckingham OUP

Cuckle, P., Clarke, S & Jenkins, I. (2000) 'Students' Information and Communications Technology Skills and Their Use during Teacher Training' in *Journal of Information Technology for Teacher Education* Vol 9 No 1

DfEE (1998) *Teaching: High Status, High Standards* London TTA

DfES (2002) *Qualifying to Teach: Professional Standards for Qualified Teacher Status and Requirements for Initial Teacher Training* London TTA

Fisher, M (2000) 'Computer Skills of Initial Teacher Education Students' in *Journal of Information Technology for Teacher Education* Vol 9 No 1

Guest, G. & Hughes, M. (1999) *Meeting the Standards in ICT: The Experience of Postgraduate Primary Student Teachers* Paper presented to BERA

Jaques, D. (2000) *Learning in Groups* London Kogan Page

Lachs, V. (2000) *Making Multimedia in the Classroom* London Routledge

Laurillard, D. (1993) *Rethinking University* Teaching London Routledge

Muffoletto *JITTE* 1996 vol 5

Margaret Ropp (Internet article)Computer Self-Efficacy

Poole, P. (1998) *'Talking about Information Communication Technology in Subject Teaching'* Canterbury Christ Church

Simpson, M., Payne, F., Munro, R. & Lynch, E. (1998) 'Using Information and Communications Technology as a Pedagogical Tool: a survey of initial teacher education in Scotland' in *Journal of Information Technology for Teacher Education* vol 7 no 3

Wild, M. (1995) 'Pre Service Education Programmes for Information technology: an effective education? In *Journal of Information Technology for Teacher Education* Vol 4 No 1

ICT as a Specialist Subject in Initial Teacher Training

John Chatterton

Postgraduate students following a one-year teacher-training course in information technology have to make rapid adjustments as to how they view their subject, their knowledge of it and their views of teaching and learning in schools. They can be helped to make these changes if the origins of the problem are understood and if the course design recognises the importance of the cognitive process and allows them to construct their own learning within the parameters set by legislation and good practice.

ICT and the Curriculum

The Origins of ICT in Schools

Information and communications technology (ICT) is still a 'young' subject. Although computer programming was taught in schools in the 1960s and there were some experiments with computers, both as 'teaching machines' and in more exploratory learning modes, the use of computers in schools remained very much a minority interest. In 1980 the UK government set up the Microelectronics Education Project. This organisation, and its successors (NCET[i] and BECTa[ii]), helped drive the expansion of interest in the use of computers in education and encouraged schools to purchase their first computers and train some staff to use them. With relatively little investment and no defined place in the curriculum, the technology remained the province of the few who were interested. It was not until the second half of the 1990s that the use of computers began to have a major impact in the classroom:

- exponential growth in power of computers, ease of use and falling costs had allowed them to become important in many aspects of everyday life
- successive changes to the national curriculum (DoE 1990, 1995; DfEE, 2000) gave ICT an increasingly important place in the classroom
- UK governments devoted considerable funding to ensure that ICT hardware, including internet connections, became available to school pupils in all phases and subjects
- ICT became a compulsory part of initial teacher training (DfEE, 1998)
- beginning in 1999/2000, all existing teachers were offered training in the use of ICT in their teaching and professional development.

Problems with ICT

Many of the problems schools and teachers face with ICT are related to its 'youth'. In hardware terms alone schools must make a major investment just to begin teaching with ICT and this investment must be repeated on a three- or four-year cycle as the technology changes. Computers which were regarded as top-of-the-range, when IT became a subject in the 1995, National Curriculum (DoE, 1994) are now obsolete. The subject matter also changes: the World Wide Web was still a new idea in 1995, now it is a fundamental part of every pupil's experience.

Teachers too face the difficulty of ever changing skills and concepts, which they have to learn and then learn to apply to their own classrooms. Non-specialist teachers using ICT are often faced with pupils whose basic ICT skills are better than their own. This in itself may not be too much of a problem but, in using ICT, teachers

> ... have greater difficulty controlling the focus of pupils' work in the classroom because, for example, pupils may have full access to all the features of the software they are using, and to all other installed software. In other NC subjects, teachers have much greater control over the texts, worksheets and other learning resources available to pupils.
>
> (Crawford, R. 1999)

Crawford also says that

> Teaching and learning IT are inherently constructivist activities, and IT teachers who attempt to implement learning programmes designed from predominantly behaviourist perspectives quickly find that these are less effective.

and that, running counter to this,

> HMI and OfSTED recommend a return to whole class, didactic teaching and other teacher centred strategies.

Teachers who are uncertain of the ICT content in their subject or its place in teaching may rely on the security (for them) of 'whole class, didactic teaching' as a tried and trusted approach. However, this may result in trivialising ICT content to the 'click this ... to do that' level, resulting in little learning and low motivation which will, in turn, reinforce the teachers' low opinion of the usefulness of ICT.

Whether ICT forms the main focus of a course or whether it is integrated into a course as part of the teaching and learning strategy, evidence of profound changes in how people learn and how learning relationships are structured has been accumulating for some time.

The Role of ICT

In schools, ICT plays two separate and, to some extent, conflicting roles: it is a subject in its own right and also an integral part of the teaching and learning of all subjects.

As a subject, ICT is separate from computer science and is about far more than developing basic skills in using a word processor or searching a database. As a teaching and learning tool, ICT must be available to all pupils: teachers are expected to ensure that pupils use ICT appropriately in their work and expected to correct pupils' errors in its use, where the need arises (NC2000). In this respect, ICT is seen as an essential, cross-curricular skill needed for effective learning in all subject areas. ICT is not alone in this: English and, to a lesser extent, maths can also be seen to play an important role across all areas of the curriculum and teachers are expected to encourage their correct and appropriate use. Also like English and maths, while most teachers recognise the place of ICT in the curriculum, they are happy to leave the actual teaching of ICT to others (Goldstein1997).

The two roles are also evident in teacher training. More than 30 universities (GTTR, 2001) now offer specialist PGCE courses in ICT: such courses are intended for people who are themselves specialists in ICT and who intend to teach ICT as a subject. Now, all student teachers must be trained to use ICT within their own curriculum areas: they are expected to demonstrate a range of personal and professional ICT skills, no matter what subject they teach. During training, students who are not ICT specialists must successfully make the transition from being someone with, maybe, a very limited experience of ICT, to being competent and confident in organising its use in teaching and learning situations. Students who are ICT specialists must learn to transfer their skills to the classroom, as well as recognise and value the contribution they can make in establishing their colleagues' ICT skills and support the use of ICT in a range of curriculum areas.

Training to Teach ICT

The ICT Students
M. Bradshaw (Bradshaw, 2000) provides a simple discussion of general and phased cognitive acts and these headings provide a useful way of examining the nature of student learning on the PGCE IT course at Sheffield Hallam University.

1. General Cognitive Acts
1.1 Orientation:
- Goal focus
- Problem focus
- Plan of action

1.2 Formulation
- Substantive
- Procedural

1.3 Assessment
- Diagnostic
- Formative
- Summative

2. Phased Cognitive Acts
2.1 Investigation:
- Examine
- Locate

2.2. Interpretation
- Classify
- Collate

2.3. Representation
- Presentational forms
- Interactive forms

from Bradshaw, M. 2000 http://users.netmatters.co.uk/pmb/ACT.html

From the very beginning of the PGCE course, we need to be explicitly concerned with the general cognitive acts of orientation, formulation and assessment. Typically, PGCE ICT students are a disparate group in terms of age, experience and educational background. Their ages range over four decades from 22 to the mid 50s, with only a few following what was once the expected route of school → university → teacher training → school. Older students may well have 20 years' experience of working in the ICT industry, but their degrees may be anything from Archæology to Zoology, while younger graduates have a degree in one of the ICT / computing disciplines, but little or no work-based experience. None is likely to have covered the full range required by the National Curriculum for ICT. They may have programming skills but no experience of control systems, or experience of systems analysis, but not of measurement / data capture by sensors. The range of backgrounds also means that the students' views of what happens in schools and what teachers and pupils do are constructed on very different experiences. Yet within a few days of starting training, they must begin to make sense of their practical experiences in their placement schools. The principal cognitive activities at this early stage need to be based in what Bradshaw (2000) calls *orientation*:

• students must become clear about their goals and the course goals;
• they must set about identifying the problems that have to be tackled; and
• they must begin to draw up a plan of action.

The cognitive process is, however, iterative. To develop a clear goal focus, students must be aware of what is required of them **and** of what they bring to the course. In subject knowledge requirements, for example, students must be aware of what is taught in their subject in schools and assess the extent to which they have the necessary knowledge and what areas they need to learn. This will help them refine the goal focus.

In recognising the wide range of needs and experience presented by individual students, we see the need to construct a programme in which students can make use of their own and each others' skills to develop the required competences. Students must be able to assess their own strengths and weaknesses and to use both to enable their development as teachers. This is not a simple task: throughout their education and working life, PGCE students may have become very adept at using their strengths and hiding their weaknesses but, as every teacher knows, school-pupils are adept at finding weaknesses! Students starting a PGCE course must, very quickly, learn to trust each other and to work with other students in a way that supports the teaching and learning of new, unfamiliar skills and techniques within the group.

Specialised Course Objectives for ICT

Not unreasonably, PGCE course objectives centre on enabling the student to perform well in the classroom. Typically these include statements which require the student to:
• plan and deliver successful ICT programmes of study
• assess pupils' initial ICT knowledge and experience
• assess gains in pupils' ICT knowledge and experience
• demonstrate knowledge of the assessment of ICT work for GCSE, GNVQ A-level etc.

Similar objectives might be written for any subject area. However, ICT courses typically have additional objectives that have no parallels in other subject areas. Students may be expected to:
• analyse ways in which ICT could be used beneficially in a range of specific subject areas
• evaluate the delivery of National Curriculum ICT requirements in a cross-curricular setting
• help develop the use of ICT as a learning resource in a school
• consider the use of ICT for pupil tracking and assessment
• be aware of financial / technical support implications of ICT use
• work with colleagues in schools to develop their use of ICT

PGCE courses are notoriously short of time and IT, like science, covers a wide range of degree subjects; no graduate can be expected to have covered the range required in schools. Nevertheless, ways must be found that allow course objectives to be met. This is best done by involving the students in the formulation of sections of the course itself.

For most students coming onto a PGCE course, education is something that has been done to them: they have given little thought to setting aims and objectives or designing a curriculum. Students also come with widely different experiences: they may have gone straight from school to an IT/Computing degree and onto the PGCE course, or they may have done an unrelated degree 25 years ago but have a wealth of IT experience in a work setting. Consequently, students have differing needs and skills and the course must acknowledge these. An early exercise for students is to map their subject knowledge against the national curriculum and two immediate benefits flow from this. Firstly, students are asked to discuss their mappings with their mentors in schools to ensure that the school experience helps them develop weak areas as well as use their strengths. Secondly, students have to pick an area of their own expertise and deliver a 'Masterclass' on this to the rest of the group. Such exercises not only make real the need for clear objectives and appropriate content, but involve the students in beginning to formulate their own learning and teaching.

As students become increasingly clear about their goals, they begin to make use of their existing knowledge to formulate a set of experiences that will enable them to increase their own knowledge and to achieve the goals set.

Designing the Learning Experience

It may be tempting to consider 'subject knowledge' and 'school experience' as two separate issues but given the time constraints on a one-year course, this is not really an option. (Currently, PGCE courses are 36 weeks, with 12 weeks spent in the university: only a fraction of this twelve weeks will be spent with subject tutors.) Mechanisms are needed which encourage or require students to share and evaluate their experiences – both those brought to the course and those acquired on it. The same mechanisms should operate whether subject knowledge or teaching experience is the issue and they should, as far as possible, be driven by the students themselves. If 'sharing' is too much in the control of the tutor, it becomes another task for the student, another time-consuming event when it should be a time-saver and a motivator.

To establish necessary relationships, the needs of both tutors and students must be recognised. Students' cognitive needs have already been outlined, while on an interpersonal level, they need to make friends, become familiar with their surroundings and establish peer support networks. Tutors must blend these interpersonal and cognitive needs if the students are to succeed. Also, tutors must make explicit common group needs, establish a sound group dynamic, encourage students to audit and share their experience and evaluate each student's ICT knowledge. A selection of any of the many 'ice-breakers' will help on the first day, but what is really needed is a set of goal-relevant activities that will have the effect of encouraging the group to work together and develop a mutually supportive attitude.

Choosing a School: an early exercise

The first thing on any student's mind is 'Will I survive the teaching practice?' The tutor, too, is likely to have the placement of students as a high priority as school availability, individual skills, travel distances and childcare all need consideration. An exercise, close to the course beginning and based around setting up the first placement, can set in train the development of many desirable traits and skills in the student group. Following discussion of OfSTED reports, league tables, value-added and other possible school measures, students search the Internet for data about schools in which they might be placed. Initial websites would include the DfEE, OfSTED, various local authorities and a school's own website. Students have to search documents for appropriate information, extract and evaluate relevant data and work, as a group, to find placements for themselves matching the various agreed criteria.

At first, students are often overly concerned with the location of the school: 'Is it easy for me to get to?' Usually this shows poor goal focus. Students need a good range of experiences in a supportive environment with a mentor who will ensure they get advice at the right moment. Students often ignore what ICT the school teaches or accept uncritically the findings of an OfSTED report from four years ago. During discussions within the group, however, ideas begin to change. One student may comment, 'This school doesn't teach IT in Y9.' Another will ask, 'What's the difference between 'IT' and 'Computing' A-level?' As discussion progresses, more complex judgements begin to be made. 'This school has a really good OfSTED report, except for IT, so …' or 'This school has had extra funding for technology, so … '. They also begin to integrate their own background and skills into the equation, 'There was no programming on my degree, so I'd be better with IT than Computing A-level … '.

Such comments illustrate the range of cognitive activity within the group. If we consider phased cognitive acts, we can see that *Investigation, Interpretation and Representation* are taking place. In the *investigative* phase, research undertaken by the students demonstrates an increasingly systematic search for data as they gain more explicit knowledge of what they should be looking for – a clearer goal focus. Much of this knowledge comes from within the student body: students construct *representations* of their findings and ideas to share them with the group. They *interpret* the information as they sort and categorise it under a number of headings. The effort to find an appropriate school also encourages the students to evaluate their existing subject knowledge and begin to recognise the demands of the national curriculum.

Finding data is only one part of the task: students have to share the task of matching students to schools. This task involves weighting data and agreeing on the priorities, particularly difficult when decisions made by the group affect all individuals within it. This process, undertaken in the first few days of the course, has been central in helping the group to bond, in generating the first elements of trust and in showing that, in learning to teach, the students are not in competition with each other, but jointly engaged in personal development.

Assessment as a Cognitive Act

Throughout the PGCE, students are engaged in self-assessment and this is seen as central to their successful progress. Their first act of assessment is diagnostic: students map their subject knowledge onto the national curriculum and from this complete a personal subject knowledge profile. (This is later extended to the post 16 curricula.) The subject-knowledge profile, prepared before their first visit to their placement school, is used to plan school-based activities with the mentor. For example, if the profile shows lack of experience of control technology, they are expected to gain appropriate practical experience in a school setting. The development of the profile is, again, done as a group activity: sharing speeds up each individual's assessment of their own subject knowledge and widens their perception of what is involved in ICT in schools. This public self-assessment begins the development of the student's application of subject knowledge to the national curriculum.

Students also monitor and assess their own progress against the range of competences set out by the DfEE in circular 10-98 (DfEE, 1998). The students maintain a personal profile in which they evidence their developing competence in planning and teaching, assessing and reporting and in all required aspects delineated in the circular. This is a complex task and students invariably have some difficulty coming to terms with the process. It is only by an iterative process of self-assessment, discussion, target setting, and more practice that students learn what is expected of them, what they themselves need to learn and how to set and meet targets.

It is the discussion that makes explicit the content and process of learning to teach. As might be expected, students discuss the profile with their mentors and with the university tutor, but it is the student group discussion that seems to have the most marked effect. Whenever students discuss their school experiences, a wide range of information, techniques and classroom phenomena are revealed: students bring their own experiences to the discussion, but gradually take on board the experience of others. Events and actions introduced by one student are typically modified and used by others, who will later report on the experience. This process clearly shows all three cognitive phases – investigation, interpretation and representation – as the students move between university and school, observing, testing out their ideas and discussing them with their peers and others.

School-Based Tasks

As students begin their teaching placement, they are necessarily involved in pupil assessment. Students are most familiar with assessment as a summative activity; they are used to having their performance assessed at the ends of stages in their degree and at work and the idea is easily transferred into the school setting. The idea of formative assessment is much less well developed. Students have to learn how to make use of the judgements they inevitably make when working with a class of children and they need to make explicit the ways in which they arrive at these assessments.

School experience begins with a serial placement and the students are set a number of tasks during this period, some of which are intended to highlight the formative aspect of assessment in school. Tasks include counting and classifying teacher-questions during a lesson segment, monitoring common pupil errors and noting how the teacher deals with them. During university sessions they report back on what they observed. In reporting back they make explicit their knowledge of assessment procedures and hypothesise about the merits of the various techniques seen: in hearing the experiences of students in other schools, they gain a richer knowledge of the range of techniques available. This movement (of ideas) between the university and placement settings allows the group to develop their ideas of assessment and make the rapid progress necessary in the run up to the block placement.

Students are asked to note, over a period of time, basic but important information about how ICT is assessed in the school:
• What evidence is there of formative or summative assessment?
• What form(s) does it take?
• Where is it recorded and to whom is it reported?
• How is progression monitored?
• How are NC levels assessed? … and so on.

In identifying and discussing answers to these questions, students have to deal with a range of complex issues. They have to consider:
• the relationship of their subject knowledge to the curriculum;
• what is really being assessed in any particular instance;
• judgements about ranking and levels of difficulty;
• whether assessments have a useful function – and what it might be …

It is within such open discussions that students begin to understand the complexities of the teaching and learning experience, the range of options available and the importance of sharing experience within the group.

Students are also expected to analyse the phenomena they observe in the classroom. The nature of IT as a subject is widely misunderstood, even by those intending to teach it. Initially students concentrate on the keyboard skills aspect of IT: they say 'I have to teach Publisher' or 'They have to learn Excel'. Clearly this is not so. Pupils should be able to analyse a given task and design an appropriate IT solution, choosing appropriate software. Analysing classroom phenomena, in particular teacher talk, is important in beginning to change the 'keyboard skills' mindset.

Students are asked to analyse the questions used by the teacher during an observed lesson. Based on work done within the university, students are asked to

> *... classify all the questions asked by the teacher according to their open-endedness and their level of difficulty: note the response.*
> *Record verbatim those questions you regard as being very open-ended.*

Students are then asked to analyse their observations and they look at questioning both as part of the teaching and learning process and as part of classroom management and control. They discuss the two dimensions in which the questions were classified and consider such things as

- how many questions are asked in a lesson;
- the proportion of closed, simple questions to harder, more open ones;
- how do pupils respond to the different question types;
- what teachers do when a "hard" question is not answered or when an open one is answered wrongly;
- the different purposes for which questions may be asked.

Although these tasks are set as an explicit event for the students, the analysis runs over a long period and is revisited often. One student's comments on the observations generally leads to the discussion of other experiences within the student group and these feed back into each student's school placement later in the week. It is, in large part, the group discussions that allow the huge range of required topics to be considered in the short time available. It is the discussions, too, which allow students to begin making the necessary adjustments to their perceptions of their subject and school life.

Supporting Students in Schools

During the serial placement, the profile development can be discussed within the group during university-based sessions, as can all aspects of school experience. Once the block practice starts, however, an alternative forum is required. Although materials and information likely to be needed by the students are on the university website (www.shu.ac.uk/schools/ed/pgceit), this is essentially a one-way transmission of data. A computer moderated conferencing system allows and encourages real dialogue. FirstClass™ (www.firstclass.com) provides a conferencing and email environment that allows open discussions between students and between the tutor and students to continue asynchronously using a standard web-browser or the FirstClass Client, which is freely downloadable.

However, given the time pressures on PGCE students, they will not use such a system unless they see distinct benefits in doing so. Initially, students are required to demonstrate competence in its use in simple tasks involving sending messages to individuals and conferences, attaching and downloading files and taking part in real-time, text-based 'chats'. This has little educational benefit as regards the course but does provide an entry point to developing independent use of the FirstClass system. Course and school information is put into conferences on FirstClass to *encourage* student use and students are *required* to use FirstClass to share the information collected as part of school-based tasks.

Experience over several years has shown that as students respond to the requirements, many of them begin to make independent use of the system: they ask the group for help, offer advice, share materials and information and, of course, arrange social events. In sharing and commenting on, say, a worksheet or a lesson plan, students can be seen to operate in all areas of the cognitive acts described above as they are helped to transform their anxieties about schools into more clearly defined problem areas or tasks.

Anxieties about class control are gradually resolved as the group begins to isolate the factors that may lead to disruption or, more usefully, identify those which aid good class management. They begin planning carefully the beginnings and endings of lessons, make lesson objectives explicit and consider what the pupils – as opposed to the teacher – might do. The use of the conferencing facilities in FirstClass has supported the students' cognitive effort directed at solving problems within the classroom, rather than using ready made lesson plans, and in hypothesising and making judgements about the quality of their own work and the work of others. A recent example of this can be seen in a 'conversation' about spreadsheets in the PGCE IT conference by the current student cohort.

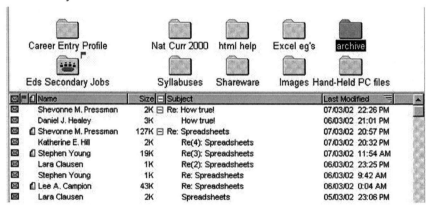

Lara's initial request on 05/03/02 at 23:06 asked for help with spreadsheets:

Hi All
Has anyone got any good ideas for teaching spreadsheets its one area I can never think of a fairly interesting way of approaching it.
If anyone has any thoughts I would be most grateful
Lara xxx

This was answered, within the hour – and just after midnight, by Lee who attached his own spreadsheet illustrating 'modelling' and a worksheet for pupils to use with it, saying

A little something I knocked up for my Y10s the other day.
It may help or inspire you. =)

Within the next few hours there were a further four contributions including another four spreadsheets produced for use in teaching placements by students in the group. The 'conversation' included one student asking

I have got to do some re-writing of schemes of work - QCA year 8 modelling one - is this the kind of thing I should be doing?

Thus the conference use clearly makes explicit the students' sharing of subject knowledge and the ways in which they begin to consider the appropriateness of its application within the classroom.

Working Together

IT staff in schools have long been expected to give advice to their colleagues on all aspects of IT from how to plan the use of ICT in a French lesson, to what is the best printer to buy for use at home. IT students too, unlike most other PGCE students, are commonly asked for advice both by experienced teachers and other students. If simple advice were all that were needed, we could rely on happenstance and the school experience. However, the current National Curriculum (DfEE/QCA 1999) requires the appropriate use of ICT in all subject areas (except PE) and at all ages. Many schools use IT staff to support the use of ICT across the curriculum. If IT students are to perform effectively in school, they need a closer understanding of the ICT problems and range of teaching techniques commonly found in other curriculum areas. Non-IT students, too, must gain knowledge and experience in developing ICT-based resources and using ICT as a classroom resource in their teaching if they are to comply with the requirements of the standards for Qualified Teacher Status (DfEE 1998).

At Sheffield Hallam, the IT group spends some time working with the Modern Foreign Languages group (Chatterton and Willan, 2001, 1999). The MFL staff identify ICT areas likely to be of interest, in terms of skills needed by MFL students and the type of activities likely to be found in school classrooms. The IT students are then asked to plan, deliver and evaluate a set of appropriate activities based on the differentiated needs of groups of MFL students. The two groups of students work together to plan and develop materials for teaching a specific language topic to classes in a local comprehensive school. After the first school placement, the groups again work together to develop resources and activities for an intensive day of language activities for an entire year group in the same comprehensive school. (The school has recently attained Language College status and is relatively well resourced for ICT activities in MFL.) These experiences have proved very valuable to both the IT and MFL students: this is shown both in their own evaluations of the experience and in their involvement in non-IT lessons on placement. Examples of the IT-based materials produced by the students can be found on http://www.shu.ac.uk/schools/ed/pgceit by clicking the 'King Ted's' link.

In cognitive terms, this 'working together' also has a marked impact. Students are forced, at an early stage, to examine their ideas of the place of ICT in the school curriculum and the range of skill levels possessed by their MFL peers. They devise a teaching plan based on their interpretation of the MFL students' needs, consider the procedures to be used in its delivery and to evaluate its impact. This evaluation is then used, as part of the information needed, to plan later sessions. Students find this activity stressful for a number of reasons. In part, the stress arises because teaching the MFL group is one of their first teaching experiences, but also because of the forced pace of cognitive change brought about by the nature of the activity itself. Not all stress is harmful. In being forced, at an early stage, to confront their ideas of the application of subject knowledge, of teaching and the place of ICT in the curriculum, students are helped to make the adjustments necessary to be successful in the classroom. The joint classroom experience has, itself, proved to be a significant motivating factor in student evaluations. Both student-teachers and experienced school staff reported that the pupils in school were motivated by the lessons and by the materials produced by the students and that the school pupils made real gains in language experience. Such positive feedback provides good motivation for the student groups – both for the MFL students to make use of ICT in their own practice and for the IT group to offer help to others whilst on placement.

In using their observations diagnostically and formatively to develop further teaching activities, students gain early experience of the basic skills needed to teach effectively on their placements. Evaluations of the work done by the students and the students' own evaluations of their work and of the PGCE course (Chatterton and Willan, 2001, 1999) have shown the value of this shared experience. The MFL group's progress in the use of ICT in their teaching is significantly better than comparable groups within the university and comments made by students within the FirstClass conference system show the level of interest and extent of help being offered during teaching placements. Course exit evaluations over the last three years have shown that the attitude of the MFL group towards ICT is much more positive than that of other student groups and their own evaluations and mentor reports show they use ICT actively within their lessons. They have clearly incorporated ICT into their teaching. In this, we can see the cognitive developments which have taken place with the students clearly demonstrating the investigation, interpretation and representation aspects of the phased cognitive acts described by Bradshaw (2000).

Beginning to Teach

The transition from student to teacher is a complex one. For most students, the achievement of the required competences (at the time of writing, DfEE Circular 4/98, 1998) means adjustments to beliefs, perceptions and memories. The process that brings about the transition calls into question their subject knowledge and changes their view of what is important. It also changes the way they view children and the teaching and learning process, and leads them to question their own memories of school and experiences of teaching and learning, on which their initial approach to the classroom is so often based.

For these changes to be securely embedded and for their continuing professional development, students need to be explicitly aware of the processes and events that brought them about. The 'discussions', referred to throughout the chapter, are a vital part of making changes explicit: they allow individual students to examine their own cognitive change in the light of what is happening to others. The changes are less threatening because they are happening to others in the group: they come to be seen not as a problem, but as part of the desired outcome. The discussions need not be face-to-face, or even contemporaneous: the conference facility in FirstClass™ allows discussions to continue out of the university and over the past few years has played an increasingly important role as access to hardware has become universal amongst the group.

For the tutor, too, the 'discussions' provide an excellent means of monitoring student progress; of seeing where the necessary cognitive change is occurring and where help is needed; of providing guidance and enabling students to take charge of their own development. Students who have difficulty discussing events and observations within the group are often those who find themselves in difficulty in the classroom. Possibly they find it difficult to be explicit about their own needs or their pupils' needs and so find it hard to plan and deliver lessons which meet those needs. The fact that this becomes apparent at an early stage allows the tutor to intervene early and to work with the mentor to give the student every opportunity to develop into a successful teacher.

References

Bradshaw, M. (2000) Learning Activities, http://users.netmatters.co.uk/pmb/ACT.html, Downloaded Dec 2000 from http://users.netmatters.co.uk/pmb/Home.html

Chatterton, J. L. & Willan, C. E. (2001) Co-operative Teaching and Learning in Information Technology and Modern Foreign Languages, SITE 2001, Florida, USA

Chatterton, J. L. & Willan, C. E. (1999) Teaching IT, Learning MFL, ITTE 1999, Amsterdam, Holland

Crawford, R. (1999) http://www.hud.ac.uk/ITsec/itped.htm

DfEE / QCA (1999) National Curriculum 2000, Department for Education and Employment / Qualifications and Curriculum Authority, http://www.nc.uk.org

DfEE (1998) Standards for the Award of Qualified Teacher Training, Circular 4/98, Department for Education and Employment

Department for Education (1995) The National Curriculum, Department of Education

Department for Education (1990) The National Curriculum, Department of Education

Goldstein, G. (1997) Information Technology in English Schools, HMSO

GTTR (2001) Graduate Teacher Training Registry http://www.gttr.ac.uk

Jaworski, B. (2000) Constructivism and Teaching – The socio-cultural context http://www.grout.demon.co.uk/Barbara/chreods.htm

---

[i]National Council for Educational Technology

[ii]British Educational Communications Technology Agency

Information society, situatedness and social construction: student teachers' learning on a PGCE geography course

Tony Fisher

Background

Teacher education in many countries is experiencing change, reflecting governmental concerns with reforming educational systems. Use of Information and Communications Technology (ICT) is one part of such reform. In England, considerable official emphasis was given to ICT in initial teacher education, in the form of an 'initial teacher training (sic) national curriculum for ICT in subject teaching' (DfEE 1998). This curriculum (referred to as 'Annex B' from the government circular in which it was set out) applied to all teachers regardless of subject. But of course this curriculum was not the first requirement for ICT (or IT as it was called previously), and it was by no means the point at which teacher educators began preparing new teachers to use new technologies.

For several years Nottingham University School of Education, in common with other providers of initial teacher education, has engaged in a process of course development to give student teachers opportunities and support to learn about using computers. This learning was seen in terms of student teachers' personal ICT capability, and also as a part of their professional responsibilities. Although the arrival of a curriculum in Annex B brought an extensive set of requirements with a much greater degree of specificity than hitherto, in a sense the underlying structure was nothing new. The identification in Annex B of two subsections: 'A: effective teaching and assessment methods' and 'B: trainees' knowledge and understanding of, and competence with, information and communications technology' (DfEE 1998) reflected two ways of thinking about ICT in initial teacher education which were already part of established practice.

This is not to diminish the impact of the 1998 requirements, which stimulated considerable activity including the reviewing and auditing of courses for opportunities to include use of ICT, drafting detailed audits for ICT capability of student teachers, and development of systematically interrelated course components. Annex B also stimulated greater priority for ICT on many courses, resulting in greater explicitness about what should be covered, where, when and by whom, and reflection on the theoretical underpinnings. Annex B stimulated discussions at several levels in our School of Education, including whole course and subject course, with teachers in local schools and at national and regional conferences.

ICT in teacher education

Annex B was not the first computer-related requirement for new teachers (for example, DFE 1992), but it was by far the most detailed and prescriptive, coming at a time of increasing government intervention in teacher education. This new curriculum represented a clear conviction that not only should pupils in schools learn *about* computers and their uses, but also that education in all subjects will benefit from teaching and learning *with* computers.

> another teaching tool. Its potential for improving the quality and
> ificant. Equally, its potential is considerable for
> eryday classroom role, for example by reducing the
> associated with it, and in their continuing training
>
> (DfEE, 1998: 1)

> y of a profound impact on education foreshadowed
> of ICT in teaching, learning and administration.

> a revolution in educational technology, not only in the
> transform teaching and learning situations, but also in
> store and process information.
>
> (Midgley et al., 1985: 14)

> refer to 'potential'?
> n has been neither as rapid nor as pervasive as in
> review of curriculum change, McCormick (2000: 221)
> be described as disappointing". Even earlier the
> fied a need to develop more effective use of IT in initial
> the Initial Teacher Education and New Technology
> ange of activity in participating institutions, findings
> to the rest of the sector. (Somekh and Davis, (Eds),

iders of initial teacher education during the 1990s was not conducive for student teachers seeking to put ICT to use when on placement (Bell and Biott, 1997, Fisher, 1996). Teachers were, at best, in the early stages of using computers in their work, though there were exceptions. From early 1970s onward there had been numerous localised ICT projects. These had reporting and dissemination strategies, but the necessary conditions for change were often not found in other schools and the impact was therefore limited.

After 1998 however, a post-graduate student teacher on a 36-week course leading to Qualified Teacher Status (QTS) by regulation spent 24 weeks in school-based work. Yet these 24 weeks were to be spent in schools and classrooms where, according to an official commentary on inspection findings, 'much remains to be done to improve professional practice in the teaching of IT and in its productive use.' (Goldstein, 1997)

Generally, schools were not well equipped with necessary hardware. Most school budgets did not allow for such spending, and where older hardware was in place, it was unusual to find a budgeted strategy for replacement and upgrading. 'Schools vary greatly in the extent to which they are able to afford to upgrade their IT resources regularly.' (Goldstein, 1997) Access to the 'IT room' was often subject to timetabling constraints as the new subject of IT began to claim preferred status. Thus, for many teachers ICT was not a major feature of their practice or thinking. The systematic use of computers did not enter the 'pedagogical content knowledge' of most teachers, that is, their knowledge and understanding of how to teach their particular subject..

Thus the student teacher going into school often found neither equipment nor awareness that would support technology use. Further, 'there is an accumulating body of research evidence indicating that the quantity and quality of a student teacher's IT experience is critically dependent on the culture of the placement school, and in particular, on the mentor in that school.' (Summers et al., 1996:156) This had clear implications for quality assurance in school-based, 'partnership' courses and, hence, for the relationships between higher education institutions and the schools with which they were in partnership. This is neither to criticise nor to blame teachers or schools. A much broader set of reasons existed in the social, economic and cultural changes affecting society and associated with ICT.

Education for the Information Society

The proliferation of computers is interwoven with the broader transition from the modern era to that of 'postmodernity'. In particular, the development of increased computer memory and faster processing, together with the extension of the Internet, have been closely associated with the compression of time and space. Harvey (1989) identified compression of time and space as key characteristics of the condition of postmodernity.

The transition to postmodernity has created tensions in schools. Secondary schools are essentially modernist institutions (Hargreaves, 1994) in 'their immense scale, their patterns of specialisation, their bureaucratic complexity, their persistent failure to engage the emotions of many of their students and considerable numbers of their staff' (p9), yet much of the world around them has become increasingly postmodern. Networked computers have enabled fundamental changes in how that world operates, but have not had the same impact on schools which are organised into subject departments, timetables, classrooms. These aspects mirror characteristics of Fordist-type mass production. However, much economic activity in advanced economies has changed from Fordism, and this has been associated with the impact of new technologies. These changes have been championed, resisted or accepted as inevitable but have not been without controversy, conflict, and unwelcome consequences. *Should* schools, undergo the same transformation?

Apple (1992), whilst not opposing the introduction of new technologies *per se* into schools, warned of potential dangers. He argued that the technological 'bandwagon' might promise more than it could deliver in attempts to enter the potentially lucrative education market. The enthusiastic promotion of new technologies might result in a marginalisation of questions concerning social and ethical impacts, such as: who gains when computers are used? who loses? who decides? The task of educators, he argued, is to ensure that when new technology enters the classroom, 'it is there for politically, economically and educationally wise reasons, not because powerful groups may be redefining our educational goals in their own image.' (p120).

Many societies are themselves in difficulty, economically and socially. Schools have been charged with the responsibility to 'administer the innovative treatment if the ailing society is to recover.' (Winer et al., 1987: 64) This view has been fuelled by government concern with international competitiveness (Ridgway, 1997:6). In the UK traditional manufacturing has declined, with a movement toward what is termed an 'information economy'. Thus the drive for education to produce a skilled, technologically literate workforce has gained impetus.

Policy-makers have attempted to create a 'learning society' for the twenty-first century. Such a society places emphasis on the individual taking responsibility for lifelong learning to keep up with changing economic, technological and social circumstances. Use of new technologies is seen both as a means to an end, by playing a key role in providing access to information and training, and as an end in itself. 'Governments in Europe and around the world have already recognised the need to review educational practices and incorporate new technologies. Their view is of a vocational imperative and one in which IT will increase the quality and efficiency of learning itself.' (Somekh et al., 1997:3)

A sequence of initiatives and changes in schools has resulted. Watson argued (1997: 82) that an underlying dichotomy of purpose between pedagogical arguments (related to beneficial impacts on teaching and learning), and vocational arguments (relating to the development of a skilled workforce for the Information Age), has resulted in confusion among teachers as to why they are encouraged to develop the use of computers in their work. Educational policies and initiatives proliferate and,

> ... as the pressures of postmodernity are felt, the teacher's role expands to take on new problems and mandates - though little of the old role is cast aside to make room for the new changes. Innovations multiply as change accelerates, creating senses of overload among teachers and principals or headteachers responsible for implementing them. More and more changes are imposed and the timelines for their implementation are truncated.
>
> (Hargreaves, 1994, p.4)

The notion of an information society has exercised a strong influence for some years and is the context in which current and recent educational change relating to ICT has occurred. The sociologist Manuel Castells takes the argument a stage further. Society itself, he argues, is changing fundamentally as a result of the impact of new technologies. Information of one sort or another has characterised all societies, but in the present case, 'information generation, processing and transmission become the fundamental sources of production and power' (Castells, 1996: 24). Others, however, are more sceptical that the change is anything other than one of degree, a continuation of past trends (e.g. Webster, 1995: 6-29; Martin, 1995: 11).

In this context the UK government has intervened with a three-pronged strategy, influencing curriculum, infrastructure and training. ICT is a required component of the National Curriculum, both as a subject with programmes of study and assessment requirements, and also as a required aspect of all other subjects. Infrastructure spending is focused on the National Grid for Learning, providing Internet connectivity and associated hardware for schools as part of a broader strategy. The Initial Teacher Training National Curriculum for the use of ICT in subject teaching (DfEE Circular 4/98 Annex B) was introduced to influence training. It also forms the basis for the New Opportunities Fund ICT training for serving teachers. It thus comprises a blueprint for teachers' knowledge and understanding of the educational use of new technologies, and a specification for teachers' personal computer capability. It demonstrates the government's belief that future education should be closely linked with increasing use of computers and associated technologies. Skills in, and an understanding of, the use of such technologies are considered necessary for all teachers, regardless of subject and are now required even for the award of qualified teacher status (QTS).

ICT in teacher education: social constructivism and situated cognition

The context of initial teacher education is characterised by a high degree of change, involving instability and uncertainty. It is also characterised by discourses which construct and reinforce certain interpretations of the role and meaning of ICT in contemporary society in general, and in education in particular. It is against this background that we now turn to how one institution responded to the challenge.

The University of Nottingham Partnership prepares around three hundred new teachers per year for the secondary age range in the three National Curriculum core subjects (mathematics, English and science) and three further foundation subjects (geography, history and modern foreign languages). Whilst School of Education staff members have been, and continue to be, involved in ICT-related research, development and evaluation, the School has no staff with a subject background in technology, and does not provide a subject specialist option in ICT. Thus ICT in the School has been, and continues to be, an aspect of other subjects, of the 'whole curriculum', and of approaches to teaching and learning, rather than a subject in its own right.

At the micropolitical level within the institution, there is no ICT subject 'territory', in which one or more individuals stand from which to exert an influence. At the socio-cultural level no distinctive ICT subject culture has developed within the institution, and consequently no history or traditions from which to offer a 'specialist' perspective. The structure of the PGCE course reinforces the perception of ICT as a part of other domains, a means to an end, rather than something which might be an end in itself. For instance, though support for general ICT skills development is provided at whole course level, progress is monitored by subject tutors, and individual subject courses take responsibility for considering the role of ICT in teaching and learning.

Shortly before the introduction of the Annex B curriculum the PGCE team undertook a process of clarifying and declaring a set of shared values (Saunders and Fraser, 1998). This collaborative process involving all members of the team was our response to the increasing level of intervention in our work as teacher educators, and reflected our desire to identify an agreed basis for a principled response to externally mandated change. One principle identified was that 'good teacher education is taught by teacher educators who... have a sensitive understanding of how students make most progress in the classroom, and because they understand the social aspects of learning they see school as a place where people can learn from one another.' This statement recognises two fundamental, linked orientations towards learning: situated cognition and social constructivism. These have implications for the approach adopted towards curriculum development for ICT in the PGCE course.

It may be helpful to establish what situated cognition and social constructivism are *not*. There is a view of knowledge expressed in cognitivist, 'objectivist' or 'symbol processing' theories of learning. This view of learning (and indeed of knowledge itself) is based on the assumption that there exists an objective reality, independent of the context in which that reality is experienced and perceived. Further, 'there is a correct way of describing it'. (Scott, 2001: 33) Hence 'the cognitive paradigm emphasises the transmission of knowledge products assuming that we can objectify reality'. (Hung and Chen, 1999: 236) Social constructivism and situated cognition eschew this view of knowledge, though 'the "symbol-processing" view of cognition, in which human thinking is seen as akin to a computer performing formal operations on symbols, has been the uncontested leader among approaches to understanding human thinking, learning and development since some time in the 1960s.' (Bredo, 1994)

Unless we wish to get into philosophical discussion on the nature of knowledge and the relationship between the 'knower' and the 'known', some level of objectivism may be accepted unproblematically. For instance, taking a geographical example, we may accept that on an Ordnance Survey map a small black square with a cross represents a church with a tower; and there would be a fair degree of agreement on what sort of object in the world a church with a tower actually is. Further, that map 'reading' includes the activity of 'translating' such a symbol and others, in order to understand what the map tells us about the 'objective' world it represents.

Constructivism by contrast provides us with a rather different view of learning based on the premise that the mind actively constructs knowledge, rather than simply receives it through transmission. Thus, in the above example, the objective 'fact' of knowing that the symbol represents the church is subordinate to what the ideas of both 'map' and 'church' *mean* to the individual. This in turn is inseparable from the individual's prior experience of maps and churches, which would have a determining influence on what might be learned.

Constructivist thinking has influenced many who have attempted to understand the complexities of the activity we call 'learning'. Two psychologists associated with constructivism are Piaget and Vygotsky but their views are frequently contrasted: Piaget's view of knowledge construction focuses on the individual (and, hence, processes internal to that individual), whereas the Vygotskyan perspective is that knowledge construction is predominantly a *social* process involving negotiation between individuals, towards shared meanings. 'Where constructivism emphasizes cognition as an individual activity and "in the head", social constructivism focuses mostly on knowledge socially constructed "in the world".' (Hung and Chen, 1999: 239). This leads us inevitably to a 'situated' view of cognition, which, in the Vygotskyan sense, is situated in interactive social processes.

Like constructivism, situated cognition stands in contrast to 'symbol processing' views of knowledge. The task of learning in the 'symbol processing' view is to assemble mental representations (or 'schema') of an external objective reality; thus, a fundamental separation exists between the learner and the environment. A series of dualisms characterise the 'symbol processing' approach: language and reality; mind and body; individual and society (Bredo, 1994). This emphasis is reflected in the well-known distinction between 'know how' and 'know that' (or 'procedural' and 'declarative' knowledge), and the privileging of the latter.

> Many methods of didactic education assume a separation between knowing and doing, treating knowledge as an integral, self-sufficient substance, theoretically independent of the situations in which it is learned and used. The primary concern of schools often seems to be the transfer of this substance, which comprises abstract, decontextualized formal concepts. The activity and context in which learning takes place are thus regarded as merely ancillary to learning; pedagogically useful, of course, but fundamentally distinct and even neutral with respect to what is learned.
>
> (Brown et al., 1989:32)

Situated cognition starts from a very different assumption. 'Situated cognition or environmentally embedded learning approaches… view the person and the environment as mutually constructed and mutually constructing… indeed they understand learning as contextualised.' (Scott 2001: 37) Context (situation), including social interactions, is fundamentally important and inextricably part of the process of learning.

Student teachers' learning about computer use, developed during degree courses and in Higher Education-based aspects of Initial Teacher Education, does not transfer easily into schools. Students' understanding of how to use technology was developed in very different situations (*this* software, *this* task, *this* setting – even this *particular* model of computer!), lacking the array of contextual variables characterising the school situation. Getting to grips with these contextual variables in a new situation has meant that student teachers had little opportunity to reflect on how to apply their ICT skills in the new situation.

Ideas of situated cognition indicate that the learning required of student teachers, even those possessing requisite ICT skills, is considerably more than simply understanding the pedagogical application of the technology (important though this is). Scott suggests (2001: 37) four contexts within which the student teacher's learning takes place: *knowledge; power; teaching and learning strategies; structures of the learning environment.*

The *knowledge context* includes general ideas about the Information Society, and more specifically the educational response represented by governmental requirements, for example, Annex B. That created a requirement for all student teachers, regardless of subject. Yet subjects have different cultures and practices which in turn offer possibilities and constraints regarding the educational use of ICT. Deeply embedded notions stemming from individual experience of what it means to 'teach' differ from student to student. Current official discourse in education reconstructs the student teacher (who is, by definition, studying teachers and teaching with a view to joining the profession) as a 'trainee'. This suggests an oversimplification: that there is an objective reality of teaching which one can be trained to do, rendering invisible the messy complexities of situated cognition. Also, there are knowledge structures reflecting specific practices in each school, and knowledge exchanges with student teachers working in other schools.

The *power context* reflects the school stratification and the relation of student teacher to mentor and higher education tutor, both of whom are in positions of power and influence in determining the legitimacy or otherwise of the student teacher's knowledge, and also act as 'gatekeepers' for entry into the profession. The ethos of a school and, more prosaically the 'staffroom culture' may impose versions of knowledge about ICT use on student teachers rather than offer them many opportunities to construct such knowledge personally. Another aspect of the power context is access to resources, for instance access to the ICT suite.

The *context provided by teaching and learning strategies* reflects the extent to which a given approach to teaching and learning is strongly or weakly framed. This includes the extent to which the 'teacher' (including mentors and tutors) determines the outcomes of a given learning situation, and the extent to which the learner (including student teachers) has freedom for interpretation of what is being learned.

The fourth context is provided by ' the structural dimensions of the learning setting itself', (Scott 2001:24) reflecting the timetable, room allocation, construction of schemes of work and specific lesson plans.

Two illustrations from a PGCE course

I have established a context for educational ICT, drawing on ideas of social construction and situated cognition and concerned with the subject's relation to the 'Information Age' and associated imperatives. I now describe an aspect of our Nottingham PGCE geography course in relation to this context. In this course, most attention given to ICT takes place 'situated' in the context of student teachers' main subjects, though some developmental aspects are supported in a more generic, cross-curricular context. Emphasis is given to observing, using and discussing ICT in partnership schools as far as possible.

The 'situated cognition' perspective requires 'authentic' learning tasks. Brown et al. (1989) point out that no one has to be an expert in a particular domain to participate in 'authentic' activity. Writing about classroom activity designed by teachers for school students, Brown et al. note:

> School activity too often tends to be hybrid, implicitly framed by one culture, but explicitly attributed to another. Classroom activity very much takes place within the culture of schools, although it is attributed to the culture of readers, writers, mathematicians, historians, economists, geographers, and so forth. Many of the activities students undertake are simply not the activities of practitioners and would not make sense or be endorsed by the cultures to which they are attributed. This hybrid activity, furthermore, limits students' access to the important structuring and supporting cues that arise from the context. What students do tends to be ersatz activity.

Early in the course, before any school-based aspects, the PGCE geography group is asked to revisit an audit of subject knowledge previously compiled. They identify an area of strength, in which they could act as 'consultant' to other group members if necessary, and an area of relative weakness, an aspect they do not feel able to teach at 'A' level (examinations for 18-year-olds). Small student groups then complete the task of creating a web page appropriate for use at 'A' level. Perceived subject weakness forms the basis of the groups: for example, three students needing to improve their grasp of atmospheric processes.

The task itself is modelled on the idea of a WebQuest: 'an inquiry-oriented activity in which some or all of the information that learners interact with comes from resources on the Internet…' (Dodge, 1995). WebQuests are rooted in a social-constructivist view of knowledge, not least because they are group assignments. 'Learning, both outside and inside school, advances through collaborative social interaction and the social construction of knowledge…[and] it is only within groups that social interaction and conversation can take place.' (Brown et al., 1989) As course designers, we hope to stimulate:

- the use of collaborative work skills at an early stage, as a context for group members to get to know one another through focusing on a common task;
- collective problem solving which requires interactions among group members. These may in turn create a synergy which generates ideas which would not otherwise occur.
- The clarification of key aspects of the task and of efficient procedures for 'getting it done'.
- The apportionment of 'multiple roles', rather than a requirement that one person perform all roles. The group has to identify sub-tasks and decide who is to do what. In the case of this assignment, each small group can refer to 'consultants' among the wider group for help with their chosen subject area. Also, the ICT skill audit reveals students' ICT expertise, so the whole group is encouraged to share expertise about web page construction.

Task authenticity comes from the clear purpose of developing required subject knowledge. Further, the task requires the creation of a web page available online to the whole PGCE geography group as a resource; thus there is a real 'audience'. The pages are also accessible to student teachers when in school on placement.

A task requirement is that the web page must contain links to online sources for further information; the PGCE students must therefore locate these. The student teachers are given the URLs of a few 'gateway' sites but then required to find, evaluate and refer to relevant material. This reflects assessment criteria for the task, which are that the web page should:

• be accurate and correct (spelling, punctuation and grammar, and subject);
• outline the key points of the chosen subject area, including key terminology;
• provide categorised links to other useful web-based sources for student and teacher use;
• be clearly laid out and accessible;
• identify teaching watch-points for the chosen subject area.

Dodge (1995) distinguished between 'short term' and 'longer term' WebQuests. The particular activity described here fits with Dodge's characterisation of a 'longer term WebQuest', in which the learners 'would have analyzed a body of knowledge deeply, transformed it in some way, and demonstrated an understanding of the material by creating something that others can respond to, on-line or off-.' (Dodge,1995)

Evaluation confirmed that this activity provided worthwhile learning, both in subject knowledge and technology usage, reflecting aspects of its 'situatedness' and authenticity. Being timed early on in the course was seen as 'a good introduction to the University network.' (Geography PGCE student, focus group transcript), and 'I now know more about computers. It was a very useful experience.'(Geography PGCE student, written evaluation). 'Some fantastic web sites [were] developed providing an excellent student resource…' (written evaluation). It usefully developed subject knowledge, '…especially as I'm now teaching the subject we did our web page on…' (focus group transcript.)

The issue of copyright when using material from other websites emerged in students' eyes as 'a grey area', both in this task and as a consideration when creating web-based subject resources in school in the future. Collaboration was a prominent feature: '…we'd share ideas… everybody was there to support each other.'(focus group transcript); '…none of our four knew anything about how to do a web page but we got through it together.' (focus group transcript.) Sometimes examples of what we could characterise as 'asynchronous, distributed working' arose, with resources and components of the developing web page being e-mailed between members of a group, reflecting students' individual circumstances; for instance '… we had two people that lived a long way from Nottingham and had to get home – so one of them in particular just ended up emailing most of it to us…' (focus group transcript.)

A different activity, again seeking to establish authenticity, took place later in the course when students spent time each week in school and also at University. The 'GeoSkills' package is a series of 'drill and practice' activities designed to reinforce geographical skills in relation to map reading. These materials embody principles of an objectivist view of knowledge in that the approach involves series of questions which have 'right' answers, reflecting for instance the correct reading of map coordinates and the correct interpretation of map symbols. Users must identify the correct answer to a particular question before they are allowed to move on to the next. Objectivist pedagogy tends to be associated with software reflecting linear information structures, and thus the methodological principles of 'instructional design'. (Phillips, 1997: 19) Such an approach may be appropriate in some learning settings, and contrasts strongly with the social constructivist underpinnings of the WebQuest approach.

The GeoSkills software was available on the University School of Education network server for familiarisation and evaluation purposes. A prepared schedule was used for the software evaluation. Students were encouraged to use the software together during a timetabled session and discuss it with others. 'GeoSkills was quite interesting... glad to have the time to have a go – with others.' (written evaluation.)

Groups of student teachers then visited a local school to observe the software in use during a geography lesson in an ICT suite. After the observed lesson there was a group debrief when aspects of what has been observed can be discussed. This process reflects the need to create meaning in *contexts of practice* in which it is 'necessary to ask what people are *doing* or *trying to do* in that context'. (Bruner, 1990: 118, italics as in the original). The debrief, though short (30 minutes) was an important component of the process of situated social construction of knowledge among the student teachers about pedagogical aspects of ICT use. Interactions between group members provided scaffolding for the clarification and development of understanding. Subsequently each individual produced a written report, submitted for assessment as part of a portfolio of assessed written pieces relating to subject aspects.

In their written reports student teachers adopted a situated perspective, in that they focused on the use of the software in the context of the observed lesson. This had the advantage of supporting a thorough evaluation of the software by adding an appropriately situated dimension. It also highlighted aspects of classroom management specific to the software and its use in an ICT suite.

'Certainly for me it identified a lot of things I wouldn't have thought of before, like how do you check all the kids are actually on task when they're just sitting looking at a computer screen... and there's just you in there?' (focus group transcript.) Observers revealed through their writing that they were alert to social aspects of the setting: though all school students were seated at individual workstations and could work entirely at their own pace, many were observed to discuss their answers with one another, showing a natural inclination to a more social approach to learning. Observers also identified a consequence of the materials design , in that some users appeared to be adopting general 'trial and error' approaches to answering questions rather than working to the ostensible geographical purpose, which was the systematic use and reinforcement of geographical skills.

Task authenticity was achieved by conducting aspects of the evaluation in school in a genuine lesson (in which the only 'unreal' aspect was the presence of a group of PGCE students with clipboards!) In the previous example of a WebQuest, the learning was situated not in a school, but within groups of learners in the discipline of geography. Because in the latter case subject knowledge was foregrounded, rather than pedagogical considerations, and also because there was a real audience for the web pages, the task achieved authenticity for those undertaking it. In both cases ICT was embedded in the learning process of student teachers, a process explicitly social in nature. In the tasks described here, student teachers were each working within their individual Vygotskyan 'zone of proximal development' in which they could take on new knowledge as a result of socially constructive processes. All Scott's (2001) overlapping contextual aspects of situatedness may be identified: a broader knowledge context provided by discourses of ICT in education and of the nature and content of geography as a school subject; a power context in terms of the requirement on student teachers to undertake the given assignments and meet the assessment criteria; a teaching and learning context, in which the assignments are framed by tutors in such a way as to leave some freedom for interpretation by student teachers working together, and around which other learning takes place; a structural context, reflecting decisions about timing and location made by tutors and mentors. Thus student teachers' learning about ICT cannot but reflect the particular social practices they encounter in their PGCE course.

References

Apple, M. (1992) 'Is the New Technology Part of the Solution or Part of the Problem in Education?', in Beynon, J. and Mackay, H. (Eds.) Technological Literacy and the Curriculum, London: The Falmer Press

Bell, M. and Biott, C. (1997) 'Using ICT in classrooms: experienced teachers and students as co-learners' in Somekh, B. and Davis, N. (Eds.) Using Information Technology effectively in Teaching and Learning, London: Routledge

Bredo, E. (1994) 'Cognitivism, situated cognition and Deweyan pragmatism' in Philosophy of Education Yearbook, 1994 (Available online at http://www.ed.uiuc.edu/EPS/PES-yearbook/94_docs/BREDO.HTM

Brown, J. S., Collins, A. and Duguid, P. (1989) 'Situated Cognition and the Culture of Learning' Educational Researcher; v18 n1, pp. 32-42 (Available online at http://www.astc.org/resource/educator/situat.htm)

Bruner, J. (1990) Acts of Meaning, Cambridge, Mass: Harvard University Press

Castells, M. (1996) The Rise of the Network Society, Oxford: Blackwell

DES (1989) Information Technology in Initial Teacher Training: the report of the expert group chaired by Janet Trotter, London: HMSO

DfEE (1998) Circular 4/98, 'Teaching: High Status, High Standards', (Annex B), London: DfEE

Dodge, B. (1995) Some Thoughts About WebQuests (Available online at http://edweb.sdsu.edu/courses/edtec596/about_webquests.html)

Fisher, T. (1996) 'Information technology and the curriculum: IT capability and the new teacher', British Journal of Curriculum and Assessment, 6, 2

Goldstein, G. (1997), Information Technology in English Schools: A commentary on inspection findings 1995-6, London, OFSTED

Hargreaves, A. (1994), Changing Teachers, Changing Times: Teachers' work and culture in the postmodern age, London, Cassell

Harvey, D. (1989) The Condition of Postmodernity: An enquiry into the origins of cultural change, Oxford, Blackwell

Hung, D. and Chen, D. (1999) 'Technologies for implementing social constructive approaches in instructional settings' in Journal of Technology and Teacher Education v7 n3, pp. 235-256

Martin, W. J. (1995) The Global Information Society, Aldershot: Aslib Gower

McCormick, R. (2000) 'Curriculum Development and New Information Technology' in Moon, B. and Murphy, P., (Eds) Curriculum in Context, London: Paul Chapman Publishing

Midgley, H. and Walker, D. (1985) Microcomputers in Geography Teaching, London: Hutchinson

Phillips, R. (1997) The Developer's Handbook to Interactive Multimedia: A practical guide for educational applications. London; Kogan Page

Saunders, M. and Fraser, V. (1998) Communities in search of values: Articulating shared principles in initial teacher education, in press.

Scott, D. (2001) 'Situated views of learning' in Paechter, C., Edwards, R., Harrison, R. and Twining, P. (Eds), Learning, Space and Identity, London: Paul Chapman Publishing

Somekh, B. and Davis, N. (Eds.) (1997) Using Information Technology effectively in Teaching and Learning, London: Routledge

Summers, M. and Easdown, G. (1996) 'Information Technology in Initial Teacher Education: preconceptions of history and geography interns, with reflections of mentors and tutors', Journal of Information Technology for Teacher Education, 5, 1&2

Theory into Practice database – Online at http://tip.psychology.org/theories.html

Watson, D. (1997) 'A dichotomy of purpose: the effect on teachers of government initiatives in information technology' in Passey, D. and Samways, B., (Eds.) Information Technology: Supporting change through teacher education, London, Chapman and Hall

Webster, F. (1995) Theories of the Information Society, London: Routledge

Winer, L. and de la Mothe, J. (1987), 'Computers, Education and the 'Dead Shark Syndrome'' in Rushby, (Ed.) Technology Based Learning: Selected Readings, London, Kogan Page

IT as a Key Skill for Teachers: the delivery of IT as an integral component of a full-time PGCE programme

Stevie Vanhegan and Susan Wallace

Introduction

Education in general, and initial teacher training in particular, is continuously undergoing a plethora of new requirements. The experience of organising teaching and learning to include and integrate IT is now a common experience for both teachers and HE Initial Teacher Training (ITT) providers. However, for post-compulsory ITT, this experience is a relatively new one.

This case study gives an account of the information communication technology (IT) training which formed a part of the Postgraduate Certificate in Education (PGCE) for intending Further Education (FE) lecturers, and is based upon the teaching and learning of a cohort of forty-one students who undertook their PGCE as a one-year full-time initial teacher training programme from September 1999 to July 2000. The students were preparing to teach in Further Education (FE), a sector of which many of them had no previous experience, either as learners or as teachers. Traditionally, FE colleges have provided an alternative route for 16–19-year-olds who wish to leave school but to remain in education or training; they have serviced the training needs of local industry and commerce; and they have provided routes back into education for adult returners, in the form, for example of Access courses which allow progression into Higher Education. Recent government education and training policy on widening participation has also begun to draw a wider range of non-traditional students into the sector, including those who need supported learning or Basic Skills teaching, where IT is being increasingly used as a teaching and learning resource.

It examines how the IT component of the course was revised in terms of content, delivery and assessment as a result of, and in response to, two major initiatives currently impacting upon the IT skills requirement of teachers and lecturers in the post-sixteen sector. These are the requirement for FE lecturers to be qualified to a national standard (FENTO 2000) and the introduction in September 2000 of the Key Skills

Qualification, which includes IT (sic), as a common factor in the post-16 curriculum. (DfEE 1999). As well as describing how these initiatives provided a rationale for the revised IT provision, the chapter will focus upon what has been learnt in terms of student motivation and associated learning and teaching styles. We draw upon students' own accounts of their IT learning experience as recorded in their course journals, and upon a range of coursework and evaluative feedback. In this way we endeavour to show how students responded to and made use of the programme's IT component for their professional development.

How current initiatives shaped the provision

The introduction of the FENTO standards for FE lecturer education (FENTO 2000), however, carried an implicit requirement that the intending lecturers develop their IT skills to a level where they were able to meet (amongst others) the skills criteria shown in table 1.

Table 1: FENTO skills criteria for FE lecturer education

A2b	Use a variety of methods for assessing the previous learning experiences and achievements of learners including their basic skills and key skills.
B1f	Ensure that basic skills and key skills are integral to provision, as required.
B3e	Offer a range of flexible opportunities for learning including learning facilitated through information learning technology.
C2f	Produce appropriate learning support materials using information learning technology where appropriate.
D2h	Identify and exploit opportunities to improve learners' basic skills and key skills.
D5e	Use information communication technology and learning technology, as appropriate.
G1f	Evaluate their own key skills against what is required in their teaching.

All of these criteria had to be accommodated, of course, within the context of the PGCE's broader aims which were about producing competent, confident and reflective practitioners who operated within an appropriate set of professional values. Behind the IT requirements, and to some extent driving them, was the introduction with Curriculum 2000 of the Key Skills Qualification (DfEE 1999) in September 2000. This meant that the PGCE FE must now prepare intending lecturers to teach in a sector where the vast majority of their pupils would be developing IT skills as an integral part of their post-sixteen studies. Since the introduction of Curriculum 2000, the delivery and assessment of all three so-called "hard" Key Skills – Communication, Application of Number and IT – takes place within the post-sixteen curriculum context of A levels, AS levels, Vocational A levels (GNVQs) and Modern Apprenticeships (NVQ). At this level, pupils are expected to achieve level three Key Skills in IT.

In education the expression 'level' is used to describe a standard of achievement. However, there is no consistency across some schemes, for example, Levels 1-4 on the

National Curriculum are very different from Levels 1-4 of Key skills. Key skills levels are defined by the QCA (2001) and are related to the National Qualifications Framework shown in table 2.

Table 2: National Qualifications Framework (NQF) (Learning & Skills Development Agency, 2001)

Level of qualification	General	Vocationally-related		Occupational
5	Higher-level qualifications			Level 5 NVQ
4				Level 4 NVQ
3 advanced level	A level	Free-standing mathematics units level 3	Vocational A level (Advanced GNVQ)	Level3 NVQ
2 intermediate level	GCSE grade A*-C	Free-standing mathematics units	Intermediate GNVQ	Level 2 NVQ
1 foundation	GCSE grade	Free-standing mathematics units	Foundation GNVQ	Level 1 NVQ
Entry level	Certificate of (educational) achievement			

Those studying at Intermediate level - Intermediate GNVQ or equivalent (for example, 5 GCSE grades A-C or an NVQ level 2) – are expected to achieve IT Key Skills at level two. One of the implications of this was that their teachers, too, whatever their subject, would need confidence in their own IT skills as an integral part of their repertoire for teaching and assessing. The vast majority of intending lecturers on the PGCE FE will go on to teach in FE colleges at both levels two and three. With this in mind, it was considered essential that they should themselves be equipped to at least Key Skill level two in IT. This reflected the requirements implicit in the FENTO standards; but central to this decision was the argument that, as intending-teachers of whatever subject, the PGCE students should be confident and capable of modelling good practice in this key skill area.

The course, as originally validated, carried the requirement that all students should develop their IT skills beyond the level they possessed at the beginning of the programme. In practice, this meant that those who had minimal skills, or were altogether unfamiliar with it, would be encouraged to gain a basic competence which was to be measured against outcomes individually negotiated between each student and the tutor. As a consequence there was no standardised bottom line, other than the requirement to "progress." Students already competent in IT, who might even include graduates in IT or computing who intended to teach the subject, would be provided with guidance and opportunities to consolidate and extend their expertise and apply IT to their teaching role. The range of student ability and experience in IT at entry had a number of consequences for subsequent teaching and learning, as this chapter will go on to show. The IT component was redesigned, therefore, to ensure that even those students with minimum IT skills had attained this level by the end of the course; and that all students had produced a portfolio of evidence which would attest to their level of skills. Those PGCE students who started out with IT skills at or above level two were required to provide evidence in their portfolios of progression from their level of skill at point of entry. This portfolio of evidence, together with tutor observations about the student's use of IT during their practical teaching, was the basis on which the student's IT skills were assessed. The compiling of a portfolio was seen as a useful developmental practice – more useful, indeed than a formal skills test. The majority of PGCE students had arrived on the course via a traditional route through education, and found it useful to gain an understanding "from the inside" of assessment by portfolio.

The diversity in subject area, as well as the initial IT skills and experience, of the FE group presented the IT tutor with problems. How do we make the IT content relevant to all subject areas, and maintain interest and motivation? How do we plan and deliver a lesson that takes account of a variety of IT expertise and still focuses on the competencies associated with IT Key Skills at level 2? The structure of the course is given in table 3. This provided opportunities of IT sessions early on in the course, and for a 'top-up' session after the first teaching practice.

Table 3: Course structure over the academic year

Location	Block	Length	IT sessions
University	1	5 weeks	3 hours/week for 4 weeks
Placement	2	8 weeks	
Christmas break			
University	3	4	3 hours for 1 week
Placement	4	10	
Easter break			
Placement	5	8	

Teaching time allocated to IT was 15 hours. This compared favourably with allocations for PGCE Primary and PGCE Secondary courses in the same institution. However, two factors generated important issues for the quality of provision. Of course, (and IT tutors everywhere will recognise this) resources were very tight. Only one IT tutor was available and one IT room booked for each 3-hour session. This room contained 25 networked PCs, running Windows NT and Microsoft Office 97, and a networked printer. Internet access was freely available and all students were provided with email facilities, which they could access off-site through any browser. Workbooks for beginners were freely available: Windows, Word, Excel, Access, PowerPoint,

Outlook and Internet Explorer. There was no easy access to scanners, CD-ROMs, digital cameras or colour printers.

We developed a strategy that we hoped would be inclusive and encourage peer support. With a staff-student ratio of 1:41 and 15 hours of contact, it seemed appropriate to enlist all the expertise available. Thus all students were encouraged to attend and to seek help and guidance from each other, both during the taught sessions and at other times. So that students engaged in their own professional development in IT, they were asked to write, and submit, an individual IT Contract early in Block 1. This contract, often only a few lines and written with guidance from the IT tutor, detailed their personal IT objectives for the course. This was intended as a guide for the contents of the portfolio as well as a means of focusing the student's own development in IT. Teaching methods used were varied. Sessions usually started with a whole-class presentation, using a data projector, but small group teaching and individual tuition was common. Students were encouraged to use workbooks and online tutorials where they could. The role of peer-support was much encouraged.

In order to make effective use of the room and the tutor, students were divided into two roughly equal sub-groups; in effect, this reduced the actual tutor contact time for all students to seven and a half hours. Groups were chosen according to total points score on the initial skills profile (1 for non-existent, 5 for brilliant). Figure 1 shows the distribution of total points scores. Group A students were those with lower points scores in terms of the way they rated their IT skills. These were thought to be relative beginners, or students who needed more tutor help and support in developing their IT skills. The strategy for this sub-group was to provide students with 'survival' skills, which would be a sound starting point for Key Skills level 2 in IT. Group B students were those with a higher points score. This group was considered to be confident in their approach to IT, to have a higher skill level and to need some guidance, but less support. This group was considered to be working already to at least at level 2. With hindsight, this was not an effective way to split the group. Students' own perception of their IT skills level does not necessarily relate to their actual skills level. Consequently each group had a wide range of student IT experience and abilities, and the tutor's view was that there was little difference between the groups.

The content of Block 1 was planned in advance. Table 4 shows how each session was split into two 1.5 hour sub-sessions.

Table 4: Session content for Block 1

Week	Group A (1.5 hours)	Group B (1.5 hours)
1	Basic PC and word processing Health & Safety	Email Internet & issues Health & Safety
2	More word processing	Spreadsheets
3	Email Internet & issues	PowerPoint
4	Simple graphics	More advanced word processing

The final two sessions in Block 3 were scheduled as workshops, where students could work on their own with tutor support, and with some tutor presentation as well as small tutorial group work. The content was based on student requests for specific help and guidance, sought by the tutor at the start of the Block. By the end of their first teaching practice, students would have some idea about areas of IT skills and knowledge where input from a tutor would be needed. At the start of Block 3, students were asked to suggest what they would like covered in their final session.

Method and methodology

It was decided to monitor the effectiveness of this provision in terms of outcomes – that is, whether it succeeded in helping the students to develop skills to the required standard, and whether it succeeded in building their confidence as users of IT; and in terms of process – that is, the extent to which the students felt comfortable with the provision and gained satisfaction and enjoyment from IT. The assessment of outcomes in terms of whether the student had reached key skill level 2 was relatively straightforward and involved the students compiling portfolios of evidence which were then assessed, together with evaluations by tutors and mentors of the students' use of IT in their teaching. Assessing the achievement of students who were already at or beyond this level at the outset of the course was more problematical, as will be explained later.

At the start of the course, students completed a simple attitude profile shown in table 5. The purpose of this profile was to establish, in a way that was comfortable for the cohort, how they perceived their IT skills in the generic applications, how this matched with their experience of computer use, and also, importantly, whether they had access to a computer at home.

Table 5: Initial IT Profile

	Non-existent (1)	Pretty basic (2)	Adequate (3)	Pretty good (4)	Brilliant (5)
Word proce-ssing					
Spread-sheet					
Database					
Electronic mail					
Graphics					
Using the Internet					
Which one word or picture best describes your IT skills?					
What's the most useful thing you have done with a computer?					
Do you have a computer at home? If so, please give a brief description.					

At the end of the calendar year in which they qualified, all 41 students were sent a questionnaire, with a covering letter and reply-paid envelope, about their IT experiences on the course. Questions were aimed at collecting data about respondents:
- access to computers and their use in their current teaching work
- attitudes to learning and teaching related to IT on the PGCE course and suggestions about how to improve it
- thoughts about how well the IT sessions prepared them for their work in FE and the relevance of IT Key Skills at level 2.

Other aspects of the inquiry demanded a different methodological approach, focusing as it did on students' attitudes and feelings, where attempts at measurement and monitoring raise epistemological and methodological issues. The sources of evidence which were used were references made in the students' reflective journals; and a questionnaire sent out at the end of the course. From the journals it was possible to gain an impression of the students' attitudes, values, and level of confidence in relation to IT. As a result, this aspect of the inquiry was illuminative in nature, and as such presented the inevitable questions which such impressionistic, interpretive methods raise (Delamont, 1978). In using personal accounts as a source of data, the inquiry takes the epistemological stance that subjective narratives – what students have to say about how they feel – can be counted as "knowledge", whilst acknowledging the need for caution on the part of the researcher about assumptions that journals can provide a transparent or unmediated window on "how things are" (Watson 1997).

In summary, then, the data gathering was designed to provide:
1. An initial profile of student needs

2. An indication of whether and how their attitude towards IT developed between the start of the course and their immersion in classroom practice
3. A summative profile and student evaluation.

Initial student responses

At the beginning of the course, students described their overall IT skills in a variety of ways from 'basic' (5 occurrences) and 'zilch' (1) through 'adequate' (6) to 'good' (2). Skill levels in the generic applications also varied with students seeing themselves most in the non-existent to adequate range, and few in the 'brilliant' rating. The interpretation of these descriptors was left open to each student. Table 6 demonstrates the range of perceived IT abilities, with more students feeling capable at word processing than other IT applications.

Table 6: Summary of perceived IT skills levels for 41 students

	Non-existent	Pretty basic	Adequate	Pretty good	Brilliant
Word processing	2	5	14	20	0
Spreadsheet	17	13	8	3	0
Database	16	16	8	1	0
Electronic mail	12	10	8	8	2
Graphics	18	15	5	3	0
Using the Internet	14	8	12	4	3

Students were asked to describe the most useful thing they had done with a computer. Preparation of their 'dissertation' (14 occurrences) was the most popular activity by far. Certainly word processing was very popular. Some students confessed to successes such as 'printed off a birthday card after 2 days of trying' and 'watched my sister's wedding by hooking up online via digital camera'. Others had used a computer and 'created music', 'produced a monthly air quality bulletin in previous job', and did the 'payroll and accounts using a spreadsheet' for their own business. One student had 'produced a training package' and another 'designed learning materials for web pages with the use of "WEB-CT" – particularly test design (MCQ based)'.

The final question on the profile questionnaire was designed to not only discover whether the student had access to a PC but also provide a tentative insight into the student's level of IT knowledge. It could be that a more detailed answer could indicate greater IT knowledge. Sixty-six per cent of the students had access, at the start of the course, to a PC of some sort. A few of the responses to this question were quite detailed, but the greater majority were vague in detail. Figure 1 shows the distribution of total points scored (1=non-existent, 5=brilliant) for the cohort.

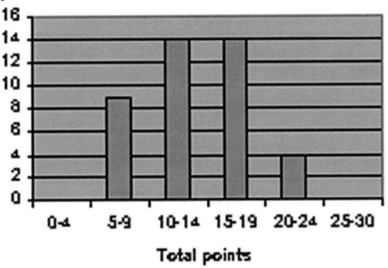

Figure 1: Total points score for each student on initial skills profile

Students' initial reaction to FE and how IT shaped their attitudes to it

The journals which were used here as a source of data were not specifically focused upon IT. As part of their course requirement, students were asked to keep a journal in which they recorded and reflected upon their experiences of teaching and learning during their PGCE course. Particular emphasis was placed upon reflection (Harland and Myhill 1997), and the document was referred to as the reflective journal. The journal extracts which are quoted here represent only a small proportion of the over all journal entries. They are chosen as being both representative and illustrative of student reflections relevant to their experiences of IT, either as learners or as teachers. Taken from that section of the journals relating to the first twelve weeks of the PGCE, the extracts provide a commentary on the students' motivation and attitude in relation to IT following their first experience of teaching and observing in an FE college.

During the first part of the teaching experience, the students were still attending university several days a week where their timetable included sessions of IT. At this stage, the IT input was causing some anxiety for the less experienced students, whose worries seemed to be centred on the possibility that they would find this aspect of their training to be beyond their capabilities.

"Oct 15
I get nervous before the information communication technology session which is silly really because I always learn something new but I'm terrified of making the machine do something I don't want it to do. Others seem so competent but I guess I am really so cosy

161

with my word processing that I don't really want to do anything else. So I've not yet filled out my IT contract because I don't know how far my capabilities will stretch."

There was some reluctance, too, to set their aims too high, even amongst those whose nervousness of the subject did not prevent their enjoyment of IT:

> "October 9th
> I really enjoyed IT today – a good lesson with lots of interesting ideas. I would like to be really efficient with a computer but I must be realistic when I fill in the contract for the skills I hope to acquire during the course and not expect too much of myself."

In the case of some students, this anxiety appeared to emerge as a negative attitude towards IT, and an indignation at being expected to push their skills any further:

> "7.10.99
> Last week I wasted two hours in an IT session watching someone move text around, so I decided I'd be better off at home. I don't need to know any more about IT than I already do. I only need it for word processing and I can already do that. So I'm not going this week."

Those students who already possessed skills at level 2 and above seemed to enjoy these initial sessions rather more than the beginners. In some ways this was counter to expectations. In the planning of the IT component of the course there had been some concern that those students who were already competent IT users might resent having to spend time improving and extending their skills. It may be that the lower levels of anxiety experienced by the IT-competent students allowed them to take more enjoyment in these sessions. It was evident, however that competence and confidence did not only or always arise from ownership of a computer, or constant use of IT.

> "Oct 6
> In the afternoon we had IT and I got put in the advanced group, which was nice. The session was very helpful. I'm amazed at the speed of the internet now – much quicker than when I last used it in 1996."

When the students begin their six-week-block teaching practice in their host college in November, the references to IT in their journals become far fewer. The focus of their anxiety seems to shift and their preoccupations now are largely with student motivation and behaviour, and establishing a working relationship with their mentors. Although the students still clearly think of themselves as learners in terms of their teaching experience –

> "24.11.99 I keep watching R [the mentor] to see how he gets them quiet and gets them working, but I think when I do it, I don't do it with enough conviction or something. I wonder if it comes with practice?"

– their attitudes towards IT become more instrumental. In other words, when their journal entries mention IT they seem to indicate a shift of focus from learner needs to user needs. For example:

> Nov 13 "Thank goodness the IT stuff here [at the host college] is compatible with the machines at the university. I can get handouts and overheads and stuff prepared on disk in the evening, and then bring it here to print it out, so I'm not paying for the paper. That helps."

And:

> "November 21st
> I just said yes I'd be able to teach that, and all the time I was thinking, Thank goodness S [the PGCE IT lecturer at the university] showed us how to get info off the internet. I can go in there and look it up and cut and paste some handouts. And it would have taken me about a week in the library before."

Summative response from students

Thirty-four per cent of the cohort responded to the questionnaire giving a sample of 14. This we felt was a reasonable rate of return especially considering our records may not have held current address details. Of these 14, all were working in FE. Eight were employed in full-time posts and 6 in part-time ones.

Since computer availability is an important factor in acquiring and developing IT skills, it was interesting to find out that only 8 had access to a computer at home by the end of the course. This represents only 57% of the sample, whereas, 66% of the whole cohort admitted to being able to access a computer at the start of the course. All those working full-time had access to a computer at work, as did 4 out of the 6 working part-time.

All respondents, with one exception admitted to using it for a range of work-related documents such as lesson plans, worksheets, handouts, exam papers and letters to students. Five respondents specifically mentioned using it for monitoring assessment and/or attendance, four for using the Internet, one the use of PowerPoint for presentations and one for spreadsheets for graphs. Only one person mentioned being involved in their own students' IT Skills qualification.

There was consensus about the use of IT Key Skills at level 2 as an objective for the course, although one person commented "I feel the climate in FE at present requires far more than level 2 of any lecturer." Another stated "Level 2 allows IT use for most basic requirements in FE teaching can be built upon in staff development sessions in post.". Ten people in the sample felt they had already achieved level 2 by the start of the course, and the remaining 4 by the end of the course.

What did the respondents think of the IT curriculum on the course? Six respondents thought that the IT sessions were successful in preparing them for it in their work. Ten respondents learned something from these sessions, while 4 learned little or nothing. These 4 also considered that the IT sessions were not successful in preparing them for IT at work, the main reason being generally that "I knew then what I needed to know". Seven respondents thought that the time allocated to 'taught-IT' was about right, with 5 wanting more time and 2 wanting less.

When asked how much they though they had learned from the IT sessions, most respondents seem to have learned something from the IT sessions. Comments included:

"Not to panic with computers"

"Basic skills"

"The order in which to do things for speed and economy"

"Internet navigation as I had never really used it before"

But one answered

"I gave up coming as it was more useful to be at home. Though I have got the handouts to consult if I need them".

Respondents proposed teaching methods and strategies that they found useful. Table 7 shows the results, especially that the most useful teaching method was considered to be peer support. This is heartening considering the vocational choice of the sample and our encouragement for them to use this method of learning.

Table 7: Teaching methods considered to be useful

Peer support (helping each other)	11
Demonstration using a data projector	8
Negotiating own programme of development	8
Exposition	4
Workbook	3
One-to-one (sitting with Nellie)	2
Workshop (roving tutor)	2
Other	0

When asked to suggest ways in which the quality of their IT experience on the course could be improved, students ticked a pre-set list of possible choices. Options were chosen to relate to a range of factors, encompassing the wider aspects of teaching and learning. The results are shown in table 8.

Table 8: Respondents' suggestions for improving the quality of the IT learning experience on the course

More tutors	8
More hours of IT	7
IT spread through the year	7
2 full days at the start of the course	6
Loan computers	5
More workbooks	5
Other	5
Wider range of software	3
Fewer hours of IT	0

In addition, 3 respondents mentioned they would like to use more subject-related software. In common with the views of the IT tutor, having more tutors in their IT sessions was the most popular suggestion.

Conclusion: The way forward

The data collected in this study allowed us to draw some very general, and tentative, conclusions about current practice and suggest recommendations for future practice, to improve the provision of the IT component of the course.

Use of the initial IT skills profile

This simple tool provided, for the course team, a somewhat superficial indication of the perceived attitude to skills for each student. Used as the basis for decision making, that is, splitting the group into beginners and more experienced users, it was not found, by the students, or ourselves, to be particularly effective. Although not currently a popular idea amongst initial teacher trainers, we have considered that, for our purposes, it might be more useful to consider administering an IT skills test at the start of the course.

IT Contract

All students provided an IT contract eventually. To some this was a source of anxiety – what to put in it could be problematic. Perhaps we should examine the possibility of guiding students with individual tutorials at the start of the course. This could be tied in with an initial skills test.

Student anxiety

As in any student cohort, anxiety, surrounding the use of computers, is an emotion that may not be obvious to the tutor. Fear of appearing foolish and of setting self-expectation too high are possibly de facto, part of the IT learning experience. We could consider ways of reducing the impact, and promoting confidence, such as more individual tuition, personalised programmes of study and formal peer mentoring activities. Students particularly found peer support useful.

Value of the IT component for vocational preparation

For some students, the IT component was clearly successful. For other students, the IT component appeared to have no effect on their IT development: not only did they feel that they had no need of it, but they also perceived that it had no value to them at all. The course team need to tackle this urgently. The course team already considered that resource constraints were having an effect on provision. Possible ways forward could include, at the students' suggestion, the use of additional staff, increasing contact time and a more informed and supported approach to negotiating a programme of study – the IT Contract.

The use of Key Skills level 2 in IT as a learning outcome

Students consider that Key Skills level 2 IT is a suitable target for the IT component of the course, based on FENTO standards and also on students' subsequent experience in FE. However, since some students feel they have achieved this already by the start of the course, might target setting for more experienced students, in their IT Contracts, be focused on level 3 – that is, GCE Advanced level equivalent in the future?

References

Delamont, S. (1978) Sociology in the Classroom, in L. Barton and R. Meighan (Eds) Sociological Interpretations of Schools and Classrooms, Driffield: Nafferton Books, pp. 59-72

DfEE (1999) Learning to Succeed: a new framework for post-16 learning, London: HMSO

FENTO (2000) www.lsagency.org.uk

Harland, F. and Myhill, D. (1997) The use of reflective diaries in initial teacher training, English in Education, 31 (1), pp. 4-11

Learning and Skills Development Agency (2001) National Qualifications Framework (NQF) www.lsagency.org.uk/curriculum2000/natqualframework.asp

QCA, (2001) Keyskills Specifications, www.qca.org.uk/nq/ks/main2.asp

Watson, R. (1997) Ethnomethodology and Textual Analysis, in D. Silverman (Ed.) Qualitative Research: Theory, Method and Practice, London: Sage Publications, pp. 80-98

Index